To:

From:

Date:

Inner Healing and Deliverance

PROLOGUE BY PETER WAGNER

Inner Healing and Deliverance

Apostle G. Maldonado

Our Vision

*To take the Word of God everywhere it is needed
and to spiritually feed God's people through
preaching, teaching, and books.*

*"I Have Called you to Bring
my Supernatural Power to this Generation."*

Inner Healing and Deliverance

ISBN-10: 1-59272-007-2
ISBN-13: 978-1-59272-007-1

Fifth Edition 2007
Copyright © 2006

Unless otherwise indicated, all Scripture quotations are taken from the New King James Version of the Bible. Scripture quotations taken from THE AMPLIFIED BIBLE, Copyright ©1954, 1958, 1962, 1965, 1987 by the Lockman Foundation. All rights reserved. Used by permission. (www.Lockman.org)

Cover Design by:
ERJ Publications

Published by:
ERJ Publications
13651 SW 143 Ct., Suite 101, Miami, FL 33186
Tel: (305) 233-3325 - Fax: (305) 675-5770

Category:
Inner Healing

Printed in the United States by Whitehall Printing Company

Dedication

This book is dedicated to my wife, Ana; my ideal helper in life. She is a vital part of my life, and of my success in ministry; sharing the sometimes trying and always exciting times.

I am truly grateful for her commitment, wisdom and prayers. I am also very thankful for Bryan and Ronald, our two wonderful sons she has given me, and whom I dearly treasure.

Acknowledgement

I want to thank everyone who helped me through the process of learning about this wonderful ministry and who inspired me to write this book.

My deepest gratitude to the intercessors who travailed through prayer and helped me birth this project, in the spirit—you are a very important ministry team, and I love you and value your input, greatly. To everyone who invested their time and talents to produce this literary work and who gave valuable suggestions that contributed in exalting the name of our Lord, Jesus, thank you!

Table of Contents

Foreword

I thank God for the ministry that the Lord has deposited in Pastor Guillermo Maldonado, making his life a channel of blessing for the salvation and deliverance of thousands of souls. Not only is he an anointed servant of the Lord whom God has been using for a long time in evangelism, as well as in pastoring, he is active in the ministries of deliverance and inner healing. God has touched him to share this area of his pastoral ministry and to put it down in this book, *Inner Healing and Deliverance*, so that these much needed teachings can be a blessing to you, dear reader. He goes even further, making these truths available to many men and women who speak different languages in other nations.

I believe with all my heart that this book, in which he expresses not only his feelings, but also his life as a minister, will impart life and edify those who are in need of inner healing or have suffered physical abuse. It will also be useful as a practical manual for leaders and pastors who continually deal with the Lord's people. The Holy Spirit is restoring all areas of the church, producing a genuine understanding and solid conviction of how to live victoriously in the daily conflicts of our souls. This is happening around the world through ministries, the revelation of the Word and the ministry of the spiritual gifts.

For a long time, many have been satisfied with the crumbs that fall from the Lord's Table. But this is the hour to receive the Heavenly bread as a plentiful gift for everyone who has the privilege of being called a "son of God." Yes, this is an irrevocable and permanent truth; for the children, it is the bread of total healing.

It is of vital importance to objectively understand this subject, since there are millions living in the valley of indecision, who need to be reached so they can experience total deliverance. Today, this inspired book comes as one more blessing from our God. It will impact every person who has the opportunity to read and study each chapter. As you read this book, you will understand those areas of your life, which need to be scrutinized and dealt with so that you may rest assured that only our Lord and His revealed truth will make you totally free. You will also be able to study it step by step and follow the process indicated, so that you may become an instrument of blessing to the people the Lord places along the path of your daily walk with Him.

Jesus said to His disciples, referring to Lazarus: "Lose him and let him go." This is the ministry of those who serve God. We hold in our hands the opportunity to lose those whom the Father, through His Son, has raised from the dead. Many have passed from death to life, but are still in bondage, their bodies bandaged and wrapped from head to toe. It has often been preached that Christ did it all, and this is true. He did finish His work, but He instructs His servants to do the job of setting the captives free. We are His hands,

His feet and His servants; therefore, we must become His instruments of deliverance.

Jesus asked the apostle Peter three times: "Do you love me?" His response to Peter's answer is: "Feed my lambs, tend my sheep." Every good shepherd must provide good grass for his sheep. Inner healing is the result of deliverance and ministry to the soul. These are good gifts that a good shepherd provides to his sheep because he loves them.

May the Lord bless you as you read this book and may you be totally edified for the glory of God as you surrender unconditionally to His will in obedience.

Jose Zapico
Evangelist

Prologue

F ew Christian leaders doubt that we are at the doorstep of a revival. It seems God is ready to release the greatest outpouring of His Spirit in our churches and communities as never seen before, but this thought is not new. For many years, we have been hearing of it through prophets and those who dedicate themselves to analyzing the times in which we live. Many of us ask ourselves: "Why has this great revival not happened yet?" We are thankful for the revival reports from different locations all over the world. Some communities find themselves in advanced stages of transformation. God is working! However, the great revival that we have been waiting for has not yet been released. I think there are various reasons why God has not yet opened the doors for the revival. One of them has to do with the subject in this book, Inner Healing and Deliverance. Allow me to explain.

When the revival comes, Satan will be furious. He will know that his end is near, and he will try to stop the revival any way he can, by transforming blessings into curses for as many Christians and churches as he can. He will accomplish this by increasing his display of demonic forces. If the Body of Christ is not ready for this attack, the revival could disappear as quickly as it comes. The results of this spiritual warfare have not been predestined. God has given us weapons for the war, but it is up to us to use them. We could make either the right decisions or perhaps the wrong ones. In any case, we will have to live with the end results of the decisions we make.

How can the church maintain the revival? One of the main characteristics of revivals that continued for more than one or two years was the establishment of ministries of deliverance from the beginning. Two of the greatest revivals to have endured in our times, took place in Latin America; these are the revivals in Argentina and the transformation of Almolonga City in Guatemala.

In Argentina, the evangelical team of Carlos Annacondia and deliverance minister Pablo Botan established a pattern of aggressive deliverance. The churches established deliverance ministries along denominational lines. The result was that they maintained the revival for no less than fifteen years.

Almolonga may very well be the only city in our generation that has been transformed socially and spiritually. A city that twenty-five years ago was filled with poverty, misery and a lack of moral restraint, today is composed of 90% born-again Christians. The last jail was closed a few years ago, since crime does not exist there any more. The farmers have prospered to such an extent that they sell their prize-winning vegetables throughout all of Central America. This process began when Pastor Mariano Riscaje discovered that he had the power to cast out demons of alcoholism. He delivered some 400 drunks in three months; this revival not only began, but it has been maintained since then.

My friend Guillermo Maldonado perfectly understands what I have just said. His local church, El Rey Jesus Ministries in Miami, has developed an incredible deliverance ministry. It is a fact that his church is one of the two most revived churches in America as far as the deliverance ministry is concerned, at least to my knowledge. There is nothing that can qualify a person more to be the author of a book such as *Inner Healing and Deliverance*.

This book will become a powerful instrument, and it will be used to establish effective deliverance ministries throughout all the Hispanic churches around the world. This book is not only theory – it is a practical manual of how to do it. If you are a pastor, you have the right book in your hands. Read it, absorb it and start practicing inner healing and deliverance in your local church. If you are not a pastor, buy another copy and give it to your pastor. If you do this, you will be making an important contribution to the revival of your city.

When churches such as El Rey Jesus multiply, the territory for revival will be ready. God will release His power because He will know that we are prepared to destroy Satan's efforts to stop the revival. The name of the Lord will be exalted and we will see our prayers for the transformation of our cities answered.

Let us proclaim the word of inner healing and deliverance!

C. Peter Wagner
Director of the Wagner Leadership Institute

Inner Healing and Deliverance

When we accept Jesus Christ as our Lord and personal Savior, we become sons of God, cleansed in His blood, and when we die, we will go directly to heaven. As believers, this does not mean we are totally free and that all our problems will end. We may still be bound to our past, struggling with hurt, bitterness or psychological and emotional problems.

If we are believers, why are we still in bondage to situations from our past? The reason is that our spirit has been born again, but our soul needs to be renewed and transformed. Therefore, it is the area of the soul that needs deliverance and inner healing.

What is the process?

The process consists of verbally expressing situations; confessing personal sins, as well as, those from our ancestors; canceling and breaking hidden powers; and reaffirming the faith in God and in His power to free us. In this process, we reclaim the restoration of the soul, spiritual healing, well-being, and inner peace. In many cases, the healing of physical ailments that originate in the spirit, are also healed.

The Trichotomy of Man

Man is a spirit with a soul and lives in a physical body. Each part of a man has divisions, which we will study carefully.

The Spirit is the inner man; the aspect of the human being that is invisible or not material. It's the spiritual nature of the man that gives him the ability to communicate with God in three areas - communion, intuition and conscience.

"20The spirit of a man is the lamp of the Lord, searching all the inner depths of his heart." Proverbs 20.27

➢ **Communion**: The means through which we communicate with God and develop intimacy with him.

➢ **Inner voice:** The inner witness through which the Holy Spirit guides us and speaks to us. It is the immediate understanding of a truth without the use of reason.

> *"14For as many as are led by the Spirit of God, these are sons of God. For you did not receive the spirit of bondage again to fear, but you received the spirit of adoption by whom we cry out, 'Abba, Father.' The Spirit himself bears witness with our spirit that we are children of God." Romans 8.14-16*

➢ **The conscience:** The means that allows us to distinguish between right and wrong. God uses our conscience to guide us to proper discernment.

"¹I tell the truth in Christ, I am not lying, my conscience also bearing me witness in the Holy Spirit." Romans 9.1

The Soul is the seat of the will, the emotions and the mind. It is this part of the believer that was not born again, but rather needs to be renewed and transformed. Later in this chapter, we will carefully examine the will, the emotions and the mind, but first it is necessary to understand in depth how the soul operates.

"²²But be doers of the Word, and not hearers only, deceiving yourselves." James 1.22

When we are born again, the work of Christ in our spirit is perfected. We our sons of God, we are going to heaven, and our name is written in the Book of Life, but our soul does not change. Now, since our soul (will, emotions and mind) was not born again, a question arises, "What do we do with the soul?" The soul needs two things: to be renewed and to be transformed.

"¹I beseech you therefore, brethren, by the mercies of God, that you present your bodies a living sacrifice, holy, acceptable to God, which is your reasonable service. ²And do not be conformed to this world, but be transformed by the renewing of your mind, that you may prove what is that good and acceptable and perfect will of God. ³For I say through the grace given to me, to everyone who is among you, not to think of himself more highly than he ought to

think, but to think soberly, as God has dealt to each one a measure of faith." Romans 12.1-3

That's the reason my many believes have emotional wounds, bad thoughts, and desires to not do the will of God; this last one being out of rebellion.

Many people are confused because they do not have the certainty of being born again. They continue to drag around unresolved issues from their past. Their true need is the renewal of their souls through the Word of God, and inner healing and deliverance. The majority of the problems that a believer endures are in the soul; in other words; his will, his emotions and his mind.

The New Birth

"3Jesus answered and said to him, "Most assuredly, I say to you, unless one is born again, he cannot see the kingdom of God." 4Nicodemus said to Him, "How can a man be born when he is old? Can he enter a second time into his mother's womb and be born?" 5Jesus answered, "Most assuredly, I say to you, unless one is born of water and the Spirit, he cannot enter the kingdom of God. 6That which is born of the flesh is flesh, and that which is born of the Spirit is spirit. 7Do not marvel that I said to you, "You must be born again.' John 3.3-7

There are believers that have not understood the new birth. The Word of God teaches us that when a person receives Jesus as his Lord and Savior, his spirit is born again, but his soul is not. The Word of God teaches that the spirit and the soul are different.

"23Now may the God of peace Himself sanctify you completely; and may your whole spirit, soul, and body be preserved blameless at the coming of our Lord Jesus Christ." 1 Thessalonians 5.23

"12For the word of God is living and powerful, and sharper than any two-edged sword, piercing even to the division of soul and spirit, and of joints and marrow, and is a discerner of the thoughts and intents of the heart." Hebrews 4.12

What does the new birth do in our spirit?

"26I will give you a new heart and put a new spirit within you; I will take the heart of stone out of your flesh and give you a heart of flesh." Ezekiel 36.26

- It gives us the ability to communicate with God.

- It allows us to know Him and His will.

   "9For this reason we also, since the day we heard it, do not cease to pray for you, and to ask that you may be filled with the knowledge of His will in all wisdom and spiritual understanding." Colossians 1.9

- It gives us the ability to be true worshippers.

   "23But the hour is coming, and now is, when the true worshipers will worship the Father in spirit and truth;

for the Father is seeking such to worship Him."
John 4.23

In conclusion, there are many believers that have to
go through that process with the deep conviction that
the perfect redemption, completed by Jesus Christ on
the cross, was more than enough to free them and
heal them from the wounds of the past.

Characteristics of the Soul

The characteristics of the soul are comparable to those
of a donkey: disobedient, stubborn, selfish, boastful,
egotistical, insecure, rude, show-off, rebellious, proud
and arrogant.

This nature must be renewed and transformed. There
are two types of life: the life of the spirit, which in the
original Greek is called *"zoe"*; and the life of the soul,
which is *"psuke"*. The soul needs to be changed or we
will not be able to enjoy God's abundant life. We
must learn to take control of our soul. The psalmist
said:

*"1Bless the Lord, O my soul; and all that is within me, bless
his holy name! 2Bless the Lord, O my soul, and forget not
all his benefits. 3Who forgives all your iniquities, who heals
all your diseases." Psalm 103.1-3*

The soul should be under the control of the renewed
spirit in Christ.

The Will: is the aspect of a person wherein resides the ability to make decisions. The human being is a moral agent, who is free to choose between right and wrong. The will is the power that opens and closes every choice in our lives, including one's thoughts, passions and emotions.

Man's will is the area that works together with our mind and emotions. It is wherein one is given the ability to decide who we want to be and what we want to do. Salvation or condemnation does not depend on God alone, but rather on the person, because it is an act of will to receive Christ or to reject Him. It is with his will that man decides to reject, accept, choose or get rid of something, and this includes thoughts, passions and emotions.

Man has a sovereign will to choose to do what is good or what is bad. Man decides to serve God or the devil. God does not have prisons in heaven; that is why it is so important to deal with our old will so as to do what God adds to it.

With his will, man is formed according to the way his culture and environment has influenced his intellectual and emotional development. These factors determine what he becomes. The man who is not restored will always tend to sin against God.

For example, disobedience is an act of our own will. The Word of God says, "The soul that sins shall die."

Why is it often so difficult to stop doing something, if we possess our own will? Because the mind that is not renewed constantly sends thoughts to the emotions that are not subject to the spirit, and so the mind and emotions try to seduce the human will. This is why man cannot stop doing the things that he knows are not pleasing to God.

God placed a barrier on human beings that even He will not cross — the will of man. The enemy cannot trespass this barrier either, so if the enemy has gained terrain in our lives, it is because our sovereign will has allowed it.

The will of man can be divided into the following functions: decisions, intentions, goals, choices and desires. Man's will is where his motives, intentions, reasons and desires originate.

Doing our own will is the essence of rebellion. When a believer does not renew his will, he will always want to fulfill the desires of his flesh.

How to Deal With Our Will

➢ Surrender it.
➢ Break it.
➢ Let go of your will and take up God's will.

How to Surrender our Will

The Word of God mentions terms that teach us that to surrender our will is a choice. Scripture uses words such as:

➢ **Renounce -** To be dead to something.

➢ **Strip off -** To get rid of something bad, such as our "old self" (sin nature).

> *"22That you put off, concerning your former conduct, the old man, which grows corrupt according to the deceitful lusts, 23and be renewed in the spirit of your mind, 24and that you put on the new man which was created according to God, in true righteousness and holiness." Ephesians 4.22-24*

➢ **Remove**

> *"31Let all bitterness, wrath, anger, clamor, and evil speaking be put away from you, with all malice." Ephesians 4.31*

➢ **Put to death**

> *"5Therefore put to death your members which are on the earth: fornication, uncleanness, passions, evil desires, and covetousness, which is idolatry." Colossians 3.5*

Remember, God does not make us do these things. We need to take the initiative to give up areas of our lives that are not pleasing to God, to put to death evil, and to rid ourselves of anything that interferes with our spiritual growth.

Starting today, you can begin to let go of all bitterness, anger and desires of the flesh. When man decides to do the perfect will of God, all God's promises will be "Yes" and "Amen".

How to Break Our Will

Our will is broken when God disciplines and punishes us as a loving father. This is also referred to as **"trials and tribulations."**

"15For thus says the high and lofty one who inhabits eternity, whose name is holy: "I dwell in the high and holy place, with him who has a contrite and humble spirit..."
Isaiah 57.15

There are three ways to know and do the will of God:

➤ **Illumination/Insight** - we understand and do His will.
➤ **Revelation** - He reveals His will to us and we obey.
➤ **Hardships** - God uses painful circumstances to teach us His will.

Always keep in mind that we, our will, is the greatest obstacle in doing the will of God.

How to let go of our Will

The renewal of our minds by the Word of God produces new desires, and since these desires originate in the will, once our minds have been renewed, we will inevitably feel good about doing the will of God.

"³For I say, through the grace given to me, to everyone who is among you, not to think of himself more highly than he ought to think, but to think soberly, as God has dealt to each one a measure of faith." Romans 12.3

"⁶Being confident of this very thing, that He who has begun a good work in you will complete it until the day of Jesus Christ." Philippians 1.6

When this happens, we agree with the apostles John and Paul:

"³⁰He must increase, but I must decrease." John 3.30

"²⁰It is no longer I who live, but Christ lives in me." Galatians 2.20

When the surrender of our will becomes a sacrifice to God, then we will be able to personally prove and experience the continual transformation of our lives.

"¹⁶Therefore, we do not lose heart. Even though our outward man is perishing, yet the inward man is being renewed day by day." 2 Corinthians 4.16

Be diligent in your search for God and you will automatically find His will for your life.

The Emotions: have to do with man's feelings and affections, that part of his soul that connects him to his emotional and intellectual environment.

There are eight negative emotions: sadness, anger, shame, pain, fear, jealousy, confusion and hate. The positive emotions are love and joy. The emotions respond to sight, taste, touch, smell and hearing.

The reality of the emotions

Jesus came face to face with all the emotions and the feelings of the human life. And He did it to provide us with resources to enable us to control our own.

The person who is motivated only by feelings, will diminish the value and importance of all biblical principles.

"6But let him ask in faith, with no doubting, for he who doubts is like a wave of the sea driven and tossed by the wind." James 1.6

Intense sadness is followed by a great joy. Depression comes after great excitement. As is the case with Elijah, who was discouraged after he beheaded the prophets of Baal. The ups and downs of a believer's emotions not only disqualify him in his walk in the Spirit, but they also propel him towards a walk in the flesh.

When the spirit rules the emotions will certainly come under control. As a consequence, complete control over the emotions is a condition to be able to walk in the Holy Spirit.

Inspiration and Emotion

Inspiration is imparted by the Holy Spirit and does not need outside stimuli to operate. Inspiration comes from within.

Emotions are provoked by external circumstances and perish without that external support.

A believer who at one moment feels like he is on cloud nine, and then at another moment becomes depressed, is an example of someone who is controlled by his emotions.

How Emotions Affect our Lives

1. They affect our relationships with others.

We are the product of our past experiences, so pain suffered in the past, impacts the way we react to a given situation.

A person who is in mourning has difficulty expressing his or her emotions. Someone with a root of rejection, who cannot show his or her emotions, will develop low self-esteem. For example, if a woman who has been abused by her husband begins a new relationship, she is likely to be on the defensive.

2. Emotions can hinder our faith.

If we allow ourselves to be led by our emotions, it is difficult to believe the Word of God, because we are always looking to base our faith on that which is seen and tangible.

As believers, we walk by conviction, not by emotion. Emotional wounds hinder us from integrating with the body of Christ and living together in love without fear of rejection. The wounds of the past impact the present and can rob us of happiness.

"⁷For we walk by faith, not by sight." 2 Corinthians 5.7

"²⁴Now Thomas, called the twin, one of the twelve, was not with them when Jesus came. ²⁵The other disciples therefore said to him, 'We have seen the Lord' So he said to them: 'Unless I see in his hands the print of the nails, and put my finger into the print of the nails, and put my hand into his side, I will not believe.'"
John 20.24, 25

Defense Mechanisms

Many wounded believers hide their pain deep in their heart and avoid speaking about it. Others use other defense mechanisms to hide their inner pain.

Some Defense Mechanisms:

Projection: When we refuse to accept that we have been hurt and do nothing about it.

"¹Therefore you are inexcusable, O man, whoever you are who judge, for in whatever you judge another you condemn yourself; for you who judge practice the same things." Romans 2.1

Self-Justification: When we justify our conduct by using the excuse that we have been hurt.

Isolation: When we isolate ourselves from other people and choose to live alone with our pain.

How should we deal with our hurt emotions?

1. **Face the truth.**

   Many times, it is painful to face the truth. But keep in mind that the door through which pain once entered our lives is the same door through which it must depart.

   "³²And you shall know the truth, and the truth shall make you free." John 8.32

   Hidden wounds, traumas, unforgiving, abuse and sins are like rotten food in the refrigerator. We can smell the bad odor but do not know exactly where it is coming from. Later we find the rotten source and discover that everything else has become contaminated. When we hide behind a door of pain, we must return to that same door in order to be set free.

2. Confess the hurt.

"16Confess your trespasses to one another, and pray for one another, that you may be healed. The effective, fervent prayer of a righteous man avails much."
James 5.16

3. Forgive and forget.

Forgiveness is not an emotion; it is a decision. Therefore, let us forgive those who offend us.

"25And whenever you stand praying, if you have anything against anyone, forgive him, that your Father in heaven may also forgive you your trespasses."
Mark 11.25

4. Practice self-control.

Decide once and for all to walk according to the Spirit and not according to the emotions. "And above all, develop self-control."

"16I say then: Walk in the Spirit, and you shall not fulfill the lusts of the flesh." Galatians 5.16

5. Make a commitment.

A true commitment means not living under the direction of our emotions, but according to the principles of the Word of God.

6. Give priority to the leading of the Holy Spirit

When our mind is renewed, the will is surrendered and our emotions controlled by the Holy Spirit, our entire being will be in unity, and God will do something new.

"18Do not remember the former things, nor consider the things of old. 19Behold, I will do a new thing, now it shall spring forth; shall you not know it? I will even make a road in the wilderness and rivers in the desert. Isaiah 43.18, 19

What is the mind?

The Mind: Man's ability to reason and to make choices, which differentiate him from all other created beings.

How should the believer use his mind?

The mind needs to be renewed with the Word of God. Before we became believers, our mind was filled with old patterns of thinking, ideologies and arguments, and we lived contrary to God's will. Now that we are in Christ, we need to renew our minds, remove those old ideas and replace them with the concepts found in the Word of God.

How do we renew our mind?

• By constantly feeding it with the Word of God.

- By meditating and focusing on the truths in the Word of God.

  "2And do not be conformed to this world, but be transformed by the renewing of your mind..."
  Romans 12.2

The word **renew** is composed of two words: the prefix *re*, meaning repeat, and *new*, which comes from the Greek root *neo*. In other words, we continually remove the old from our mind and replace with it with the new - the Word of God.

What is the body?

The Body is the seat of all desires and natural passions. It projects the spirit and soul to the outside world.

With this in mind, we could say that man is a spirit with a soul, and lives in a physical body.

By studying the different parts of man (spirit, soul and body), and recognizing that only the spirit is born again, and that the soul (will, emotions and mind) need to be renewed, we understand the need for inner healing.

- Our will should be surrendered, let go and broken to do the will of God.

- The emotions should be restored and healed so that wounds from the past are no longer present.

- The mind needs to be constantly renewed, being fed the Word of God. This way effective spiritual growth takes place in the entire being and the believer attains to the fullness of Christ, the perfect man.

In conclusion, believers can go through this process with the assurance and deep conviction that the perfect redemption of Christ on the cross was sufficient to free and to heal them of wounds from the past.

CHAPTER
ᖇᖇᖇ 2 ᖇᖇᖇ

Inner Healing

Not all believers have appropriated the total redemption that Jesus Christ accomplished on the cross of Calvary. His works encompass salvation, deliverance, inner healing, and physical healing.

"¹⁸The Spirit of the LORD is upon Me, because He has anointed me to preach the gospel to the poor; he has sent me to heal the brokenhearted, to proclaim liberty to the captives and recovery of sight to the blind, to set at liberty those who are oppressed." Luke 4.18

Unfortunately, when we speak of inner healing, some people think we are referring to psychology. This is not the case.

What is inner healing?

It is the process through which a person is delivered and healed from past traumas and pain produced by others. These traumas and pain hinder them from enjoying Christ's abundant life.

Inner healing implies a transformation and renovation of our soul -- the will, emotions and mind -- through the Word of God and the Holy Spirit.

Inner healing is not:

It is not dwelling on our past or our sins, but rather it is the confession of our sins in order to be healed. Inner healing has nothing to do with the world's psychology.

Jesus paid the price in full.

Jesus' work on the cross of Calvary accomplished much more than pardon for our sins. He also paid for the redemption of our entire being -- spirit, soul and body. Believers who are not walking in complete freedom have yet to appropriate the works of our Lord or to understand the truth of *2 Corinthians 5.17*:

"¹⁷Therefore, if anyone is in Christ, he is a new creation; old things have passed away; behold, all things have become new."

Some of us believe that once we receive Christ as our Lord and Savior, all of our problems are over and everything is made new. The question is, in what part of our being was everything made new? Our spirit was renewed, but the soul and the body are the same. Once we receive Christ, the Holy Spirit begins the process of healing us of past pains. It is at this point that inner healing becomes effective in our life through the Word of God.

The Word of God says Jesus paid the price to free all of our entire being -- spirit, soul and body.

As the second Adam, Christ came to free us from our original sin. His blood is effective and powerful enough to also cleanse us of our daily sins.

The purpose of inner healing is to be set free from past traumas. The present must be lived free of sin. Without holiness, no one will see the Lord. Peter knew there was unrighteousness within him, but this has nothing to do with inner healing.

"18The Spirit of the Lord is upon me, Because He has anointed me to preach the good news to the poor. He has sent me to proclaim freedom to the prisoners, and recovery of sight to the blind; to release the oppressed." Luke 4.18

The word broken means to be in pieces. A broken heart is crushed into small pieces due to pain. Jesus came to this world to take each one of those pieces of our heart and everything else in our life that was broken and to put them back together again. He came to heal all of our wounds, rejection, bitterness, lack of forgiveness, guilt, and anything else that is impacting you life in a negative way.

Why do we need inner healing?

Many believers, who have been born again, will go to heaven, are children of God, and have the Holy Spirit living within. Nevertheless, they are still bound to the past, and bear its pain. We fall prey to bad habits, depression, feelings of rejection, sexual bondages, fear and insecurities. We still drag around generational curses and have the tendency to feel inferior to others. This is why we need inner healing and deliverance.

The importance of facing the truth

"³¹Then Jesus said to those Jews who believed Him, "If you abide in My word, you are My disciples indeed. ³²And you shall know the truth, and the truth shall make you free." John 8.31, 32

When we hide behind the door of wounded emotions, we need to go back through that same door in order to be set free. Are we hiding because the truth is painful? Each area to be freed requires for us to confront a painful truth, and this will always cause pain. It is essential for us to keep in mind that any hidden pain, traumas and sin, are like rotten food in a refrigerator, we perceive there is a bad odor coming from it, but cannot pinpoint exactly where it is coming from, though we are sure it is coming from somewhere inside our refrigerator. Eventually this odor will contaminate the rest of the food.

What is the purpose of inner healing?

Inner healing is directly related to a person's past.

There is no **time or space** in the emotions. That which affected a person in the past, either during childhood or as an adult, is still in force in the present. There is a saying in the secular world that says: **"time heals all wounds."** But this is not true; Jesus is the only one who is able to heal the brokenhearted. Jesus Christ paid the full price for those of us who go to him with our past emotional wounds. He heals us and delivers us completely.

"¹Who has believed our report? And to whom has the arm of the LORD been revealed? ²For He shall grow up before Him as a tender plant, and as a root out of dry ground. He has no form or comeliness; and when we see Him, there is no beauty that we should desire Him. ³He is despised and rejected by men, a Man of sorrows and acquainted with grief. And we hid, as it were, our faces from Him; he was despised, and we did not esteem Him. ⁴Surely He has borne our griefs and carried our sorrows; yet we esteemed Him stricken, smitten by God, and afflicted. ⁵But He was wounded for our transgressions, he was bruised for our iniquities; the chastisement for our peace was upon Him, and by His stripes we are healed." Isaiah 53.1-5

The stages of our lives in which we were wounded include: the prenatal years, during childhood, during adolescence, during the adult years and during the stage of marriage.

The Word of God says in *Genesis 3.15,* *"¹⁵And I will put enmity between you and the woman, and between your seed and her seed; he shall bruise your head, and you shall bruise his heel."*

The enemy desires to harm people in as many ways as possible and at every stage of their lives. If he attacked our Lord Jesus Christ, he will certainly attack others.

We have all been hurt at some point in our lives, and we need to understand that coming to Jesus is only the beginning. Our wounds will not be healed automatically. This implies that there is a process called Inner Healing and deliverance, which restores us of all our past. Neither can we hope that time will heal us, because this will not happen. Only inner healing by the Word of God and the Anointing of the Holy Spirit can set us free. Amen!

CHAPTER

3

Lack of Forgiveness

L ack of forgiveness is of one of the biggest problems in the body of Christ, today. As a consequence, there are many wounded believers who
in turn hurt others. Not forgiving is an open door for
the enemy to destroy our spiritual, emotional and
physical lives.

What is forgiveness?

To forgive is to loosen, and to set free from all debt,
anyone who hurts and offends us; to make the decision to forgive is an act of will and is not based on
emotions.

*"35So my heavenly Father also will do to you if each of you,
from his heart, does not forgive his brother his trespasses."*
Matthew 18.35

What forgiveness is not...

To forget or ignore grievances and sweep them under
the rug, to deny the fact that we have been hurt, to try
to let time erase these wounds and offenses, to make
excuses, or to say, "I forgive you" without genuinely
doing it.

Forgiveness is not an option, but rather a command from the Lord.

"14For if you forgive men their trespasses, your heavenly Father will also forgive you." Matthew 6.14

Lack of forgiveness is bait for the enemy.

"6But whoever causes one of these little ones who believe in me to sin, it would be better from him if a millstone were hung around his neck, and he were drowned in the depth of the sea. 7Woe to the world because of offenses! For offenses must come, but woe to that man by whom the offense comes!" Matthew 18.6, 7

Jesus said offenses were necessary. The word offense is very significant. It comes from the Greek word "*skandalo*", which means a trap or bait. This word was used in ancient times to describe a curved, flexible stem with bait used to trap animals.

In other words, every time someone offends or hurts us, it could be a trap or bait from the enemy to make us bitter and cause us to miss out on our blessings. As believers, we need to learn how to block out offenses through love, keeping in mind that love does not rejoice in iniquity. When we are offended, it is not always someone else's fault. Many times it is our own. What is the root of most offenses? -- Insecurity and immaturity. This causes people to become easily offended, and to take everything personally.

The Consequences of not Forgiving

➤ **It is an act of disobedience to God.**

Forgiveness is an act of our will. We decide to forgive because it is God's command, therefore, if we do not forgive, we will not be forgiven.

"13And you, being dead in your trespasses and the uncircumcision of your flesh, He has made alive together with Him, having forgiven you all trespasses, 14having wiped out the handwriting of requirements that was against us, which was contrary to us. And He has taken it out of the way, having nailed it to the cross."
Colossians 2.13, 14

➤ **The enemy gains an advantage in our lives.**

When we choose not to forgive, we open a door for the enemy to enter our lives and destroy our homes, finances, health, and other areas.

"11For what man knows the things of a man except the spirit of the man which is in him? Even so no one knows the things of God except the Spirit of God."
1 Corinthians 2.11

"27nor give place to the devil." *Ephesians 4.27*

"12And forgive us our debts, as we forgive our debtors."
Matthew 6.12

Many people do not know how to forgive because they have not forgiven themselves for things they did in the past. It is important to understand that God forgives those of us who genuinely repent.

➤ **Our prayers are hindered.**

Lack of forgiveness cuts off our communication with God, and causes His presence not to flow in us.

"25And whenever you stand praying, if you have anything against anyone, forgive him, that your Father in heaven may also forgive you your trespasses." Matthew 11.25

Jesus exhorts us to leave whatever we are doing and first settle our debts with those who offend us.

➤ **God will not accept our offerings.**

Every offering to God is a living sacrifice; therefore, God cannot receive a sacrifice that comes from an unforgiving heart because that would be an abomination to Him. As believers, we wonder why we do not prosper even though we tithe and give offerings. We need to analyze our lives to see if we lack forgiveness against someone in our hearts.

"23Therefore if you bring your gift to the altar, and there remember that your brother has something against you." Matthew 5.23

➢ **God will deliver us to the tormentors (demons).**

Lack of forgiveness is one of the biggest attractions for demons. Demons will always remind us of what we did in the past in order to torment us.

The word "tormentors" comes from the Greek word *"basanistes"*, which are actually demons. If God delivers us to them, He is the only one who can set us free.

"35So My heavenly Father also will do to you if each of you, from his heart, does not forgive his brother his trespasses." Matthew 18.35

➢ **Faith is annulled.**

It is difficult to believe in God when we are hurting. Faith and resentment cannot flow from the same fountain at the same time. As much as we try to believe or confess the Word, faith will not be activated in our heart. Lack of forgiveness blocks our heart from believing in Him.

➢ **Love is annulled.**

Not forgiving cuts the flow of God's love through us, making it impossible for us to love and hate at the same time. So if offenses are not properly dealt with, God's love will not flow in its fullness. A spouse may say, "I do not love him or her any more." This is often not a matter of not loving the other person anymore, but of having been hurt so much that choosing not to forgive mistakenly deceives us, making us think that our love for the other person has ended. **The person who does not forgive will always suffer great loss, and great pain will be afflicted, not upon others, but upon himself.**

> ➤ **God does not forgive us.**

If we do not forgive those who hurt us, neither will God forgive us. If we refuse to forgive, the Lord will put us against the wall by withholding His forgiveness from us. God overlooks some faults, especially when we are immature, but He will never allow us not to forgive.

Consequences for not forgiving

Lack of forgiveness causes resentment, bitterness and hate, which result in a scarred and defiled conscience.

How can we forgive and forget?

God forgives and forgets. He has the ability to erase our transgressions from His memory, but we do not have that ability; He must deal with our hearts. We may remember what others have done to us, but if we forgive them, these memories will no longer cause us pain. Therefore, to forget means not to attribute importance to past events. We may remember, because we cannot forget, but the memory of it, no longer hurts. Amen!

Steps to forgive

1. We must make the decision to forgive with all of our heart.

Remember, if we wait until we feel something in order to forgive, we will never feel it because forgiveness is not based on feelings, but on the commitment to obey God and His Word.

"*35So My heavenly Father also will do to you if each of you, from his heart, does not forgive his brother his trespasses." Matthew 18.35*

2. Make a list of all the people and situations that have hurt you.

3. Repent for not forgiving from your heart and for the sin of judgment.

The Word of God mandates that we get rid of all ill-feelings, bitterness, and hatred, and to recognize our lack of forgiveness towards others.

4. Express your pardon verbally.

"*16Confess your trespasses to one another, and pray for one another, that you may be healed. The effective, fervent prayer of a righteous man avails much." James 5.16*

5. Renounce every spirit of resentment, bitterness, hate and for not forgiving.

Confess your forgiveness to each of the people involved and specify the reasons why you are forgiving them.

You can and must forgive. Do so repeating the following out loud and with all your heart:

"Lord: I forgive (name the person) _____ because: (In detail, list the reasons, how they made you feel when they hurt you.)"

After you have forgiven each person for every painful memory or event, finish by praying aloud:

"Lord, I present all these people to you and I surrender my right for vengeance. I choose not to cling to bitterness or anger and I ask the Holy Spirit to heal me of my hurt feelings. I ask this in the name of Jesus Christ. Amen!"

Questions about forgiveness:

1. How do we know if we have forgiven?

    When we remember what others have done, but the memory of it no longer hurts us or causes us pain.

2. How should we treat those who do not accept our forgiveness?

    Once we ask for forgiveness, if a person does not want to forgive, it becomes a problem between that person and God. The only thing to do is to pray for them.

3. How should we treat those who continually offend us?

    It is necessary to forgive them every time they hurt us. Jesus said, "we must forgive 70 times seven." In this case, it may be best not to keep company with such people in order to avoid being hurt over and over again.

    "21 Then Peter came to Him and said, "Lord, how often shall my brother sin against me, and I forgive him? Up to seven times? 22Jesus said to him, "I do not say to you, up to seven times, but up to seventy times seven." Matthew 18:21, 22

    Let us remember that forgiveness is a way of life, but the fact that we forgive does not mean we have to remain close friends. If a person continually hurts us, it may be best to keep our distance, if possible.

    Bear in mind that maintaining this distance or separation in order to avoid being hurt over and over again should be done in love. Those we love most are usually the ones who hurt us the most, because they are the closest to us.

Never forget that in this world, in one way or another, we will be hurt. We must to learn to forgive and forget, and as we follow this principle, we will mature in the things of God. Lets not forget the steps we must take in order to remain determined to practice forgiveness, and lets make it a part of our daily life, never doubting that we will always be victorious in the name that is above all names, Jesus Christ.

CHAPTER

❧❧❧ 4 ❧❧❧

The Root
of Bitterness

The root of bitterness is a primary reason why believers feel miserable, physically ill and separated from God's grace. It is stronger than not forgiving, producing one of the biggest reasons believers feel miserable, sick, and separated from God's grace. It produces wrath, anger, and swearing. It is also an open door for unclean, tormenting spirits.

"15Looking carefully lest anyone fall short of the grace of God; lest any root of bitterness springing up cause trouble, and by this many become defiled." Hebrews 12.15

"30And do not grieve the Holy Spirit of God, by whom you were sealed for the day of redemption. 31Let all bitterness, wrath, anger, clamor, and evil speaking be put away from you, with all malice. 32And be kind to one another, tenderhearted, forgiving one another, even as God in Christ forgave you." Ephesians 4.30-32

What is the root of bitterness?

Bitterness is an anguish of the soul that makes the person sad, discouraged, and desperate, the person also feels a sense of hopelessness, and easily becomes a victim of deception. The soul feels this way in response to overwhelming circumstances. It is a deep sadness and resentment accompanied by hostility and repressed anger.

Bitterness is resentment that turns into venom, contaminating and spreading throughout the soul, until it destroys the life of God within us, thus negatively impacting our personality. If bitterness is left unchecked, it can destroy our life.

Bitterness is the only contamination that makes us completely forget the good work God and others have done, not only in us, but also for us. The root of bitterness is the fertilized seedbed of the enemy. It is there that he takes advantage of the believer. That is a strong reason why believers who want to walk in victory should remain in a continual spirit of forgiveness.

If left untreated, bitterness will develop and:

➢ Grow
➢ Accumulate
➢ Mature

Because the roots of resentment grow secretly, they are able to spread deeper and deeper into the heart of man until they choke his soul. This cycle of growth eventually becomes a great tree of bitterness, pro-ducing evil fruit such as resentment, wrath and jealousy. Bitterness is easy to see in others, but very difficult to see in ourselves.

What causes bitterness?

1. When someone or something is taken from us.

For example: Naomi lost her husband and her three sons.

Every time something important is taken away from us, the enemy sends a spirit of bitterness against us. Naomi had a root of bitterness against God because she thought God had taken her husband and her three sons from her. Many believers have roots of bitterness because they are dissatisfied with God. Let me point out that God is the author of every good gift; He is not the author of evil. The person with a root of bitterness is able to live this way all of his life, always focusing and talking about what was done to him and what was taken away.

"13Would you wait for them till they were grown? Would you restrain yourselves from having husbands? No, my daughters; for it grieves me very much for your sakes that the hand of the Lord has gone out against me." Ruth 1.13

Example: When Esau realized he had lost his birthright, great bitterness came over him. *(Genesis 27. 34-40)*

2. Facing circumstances we cannot change.

When we face overwhelming circumstances that we cannot control, it makes us feel discouraged, anguished, desperate, and a sense of hopelessness. At such moments, we need to meditate on God's promises and the hope we have in Christ. When we are subjected to a difficult problem and are unable to see changes, we are in danger of being under attack by a spirit of bitterness.

A bitter person is likely to say: "I give up because there is no hope for change."

3. When someone hurts us.

One reason for bitterness in our lives is wounds from the past. When we are offended, we should immediately forgive and not let the sun go down on our anger, the situation must be dealt with and our heart healed as soon as possible.

Being aware of the cycle of emotional pain helps us to overcome difficult moments.

> Offenses
> Lack of forgiveness
> Resentment
> The root of bitterness
> Hatred
> A seared conscience

What are the signs that show the root of bitterness in a person?

- When he or she is constantly complaining about circumstances or relationships.

  "22So Moses brought Israel from the Red Sea; then they went out into the wilderness of Shur. And they went three days in the wilderness and found no water. 23Now when they came to Marah, they could not drink the waters of Marah, for they were bitter. Therefore the name of it was called Marah. 24And the people complained against Moses, saying, "What shall we drink? 25So he cried out to the Lord, and the Lord showed him a tree. When he cast it into the waters, the waters were made sweet. There He made a statute and an ordinance for them, and there He tested them."
  Exodus 15.22-25

- The person is constantly angry or swearing.

  "30And do not grieve the Holy Spirit of God, by whom you were sealed for the day of redemption. 31Let all bitterness, wrath, ire, clamor, and evil speaking be put away from you, with all malice." Ephesians 4.30, 31

- The root of bitterness becomes a registry for the offenses we receive, especially when we remember and constantly rehearse details such as troubling names, words or circumstances.

- Isolation. When we have a root of bitterness, the tendency is to isolate ourselves because we are afraid of being hurt again.

Consequences of the root of bitterness

- Bitterness can separate us from Christ and from our faith. This is an unacceptable risk.

  "15Looking carefully lest anyone fall short of the grace of God; lest any root of bitterness springing up cause trouble and by this many become defiled." Hebrews 12.15

- Many physical diseases, including arthritis, ulcers, cancer, insomnia, migraines and back pain, are caused by bitterness.

- Bitterness confines us to a prison.

  "23For I see that you are poisoned by bitterness and bound by iniquity." Acts 8.23

Many believers today feel confined in financial and family prisons. This is due to the bitterness in their souls. Bitterness makes them forget all the goodness they have received from God and from others. It takes over, it blinds them, and it does not allow them to recognize what is good in people. They tend to believe they are right all the time and everyone else is wrong.

How do we get rid of the root of bitterness?

- Find the good in every bad thing that has happened.

> "*18Why is my pain perpetual and my wound incurable, which refuses to be healed. Will you surely be to me like an unreliable stream? As waters that fail? 19Therefore thus says the Lord: "If you return, then I will bring you back; you shall stand before me; if you take out the precious from the vile, you shall be as My mouth; Let them return to you, But you must not return to them."* Jeremiah 15.18, 19

God says to Jeremiah: If you look at what is good and precious, I will take out that which is bad, and you will come out of your painful situation. Even if it I did not send you the problem, I can turn it into something precious. This will help you to mature, and keep in mind that I can take that painful situation and convert it into a blessing.

We will never be healed from pain, set free from a difficult circumstance, desperation, or the wounds inflicted by others, if we cannot see. What do we need to see? That God will bring something precious out of anything that is negative. God has the power and the authority to do it.

- We must make the decision to forgive everyone who hurts us, and to ask God and those we hurt to forgive us also.

- Make a list of people who have hurt you or taken something from you.

- Express your forgiveness as an audible form of confession.

  Please be specific with each word or circumstance in which you were hurt, defrauded or overwhelmed.

- Repent for the sin of judging the person who hurt you, and of any negative attitudes you may have towards God.

  Keep in mind that lack of forgiveness and having bitterness in our lives, leads to judging others, and that is a sin that opens doors to the enemy.

  Repeat this prayer:

  Father, in the name of Jesus, I renounce all roots of bitterness in my life and cancel all the consequences of keeping them in my heart. I forgive (Name of person) _____, For_____. Lord, I surrender all my pain and the wounds that were opened when I was hurt, right now. I give up the right of revenge.

On the contrary, I bless everyone who has hurt me. Lord, I renounce every root of bitterness, wrath, hatred, resentment, cursing or jealousy and I declare that I am set free in your name. Amen!
Bitterness can have terrible effects on our life. We must learn to be forgiving, to trust in the Lord, and to rely on Him to change the circumstances we cannot change on our own.

If we lose something, the Lord will give it back to us one way or another, but we must never allow that loss to cause a root of bitterness within us. God has beautiful things in store for us. Nothing should hold us back from continually marching forward, as Jesus Christ is right there to help us. Amen!

CHAPTER
∾∾∾ 5 ∾∾∾

Rejection

Our basic needs are satisfied by love, respect, acceptance and security, but the root of rejection hinders us from receiving these benefits because we are needy for love.

Rejection is the master plan of the enemy.

The enemy uses rejection to destroy an large part of the Body of Christ. He steals away our opportunity to be used by God and to receive His blessings. At one time or another, all of us have faced some form of rejection.

Rejection is seldom recognized or diagnosed as a problem.

People of all nationalities and races face some form of rejection. In many cases, overcoming bitter experiences is the greatest challenge a person has to endure.

What causes rejection?

1. Rejection in the womb

Children suffer rejection even when they are still in their mothers' wombs; this is because they are spiritual beings able to perceive their mother's emotional problems. Any woman who becomes pregnant through rape, incest, adultery or fornication, carry unwanted pregnancies, thus passing on to her unborn child the feeling of rejection.

Any circumstance and attitude a pregnant woman feels or experiences towards her unborn child will influence the baby while still in the womb. This is especially true when there is a sex preference on the part of the father or mother. If the parents express a strong preference for the child to be a boy or a girl and the child does not meet this expectation, it will cause rejection. Sometimes, problems during childbirth will also cause rejection.

2. Rejection during one's childhood

A child's security is acquired during the first six years of life. During this time, the child develops his values, his security and his identity. The following are causes of rejection in childhood:

➤ A lack of attention and care from the parents
➤ Adoption
➤ Children with physical disabilities
➤ Comparison of siblings
➤ Harsh or outspoken parental criticism
➤ Physical, emotional or sexual abuse

- Parents' lack of interest in protecting or listening to their children
- Over-protection
- Lack of love, affection or praise
- Excessive control and manipulation
- Abandonment
- Substitution of material things for love
- A broken home or divorce
- Birth abnormalities or defects

3. Rejection during adolescence

In many cases, a child growing up into his teenage years will experience different types of rejection. The following list provides us with events, attitudes, or behaviors that can cause rejection in a child's life during his adolescent years:

- Excessive discipline
- Mental, physical or sexual abuse by parents, friends, teachers or other children
- Pressure from others to be the best
- Bribery for improved grades
- Shaming the child in front of others
- Family poverty
- Overloading children with housework
- Controlling parents
- Pushing children to go beyond their ability and control

4. Rejection during adulthood

➢ Guilt over an unwanted pregnancy
➢ Abortion, regardless of whether it was planned or not
➢ The inability to cope with the low self-esteem of others
➢ Shame due to a physical deformity
➢ Financial disasters
➢ Isolation from the family or being sent away
➢ Inability to communicate effectively

5. Rejection during marriage

➢ Death of a partner
➢ Divorce
➢ Infidelity by one of the partners
➢ Mental, physical or sexual cruelty
➢ Inability to have children

Regardless of what causes rejection, it will affect our relationships with God, our family, our brothers and sisters, and every other interpersonal relationship we are involved in.

Some of us perceive God the same way we perceive our parents. Many times we do not feel worthy of getting close to our Heavenly Father because we automatically expect to be rejected, just as we were at home.

Rejected parents produce rejected children. Parents who have been victims of the spirit of rejection prior to their marriage will be unable to freely love their children.

There are three types of rejection, which have different symptoms:

1. **The root of rejection produces aggressive reactions.**

   Those who feel rejected tend to:

   - **Refuse to be comforted or embraced.** Someone who suffers from rejection does not like to be touched physically or to express physical love.

   - **Experience rejection from others.** People who feel rejected need time to vent their feelings, and if not allowed that time, their attitudes will cause others to reject them.

   - **Show emotional harshness.** When people are rejected, they tend to be cold, lacking sensitivity, introspective, and selfish. They often use their most powerful weapon, their tongue.

   - **Be skeptic, doubtful and lack belief.** A person who feels rejected loses faith in family, friends and people in general. He also becomes suspicious of everyone, questioning their true motives.

- **Be stubborn.** When stubborn people are determined to do something, no one can persuade them to change their mind. They will not consider other's opinion or advice.

- **Demonstrate aggressive attitudes.** They react angrily to protect themselves from being rejected.

- **Hold thoughts of vengeance.** Victims of rejection can become resentful to the point of considering or planning acts of revenge against those who hurt them, regardless of any guilt they may experience afterward.

- **Swear and use dirty language**. A great number of people who suffer from rejection use obscenities when they are under pressure.

- **Be argumentative.** Often, their arguments make no sense, but they do it because it makes them feel better. However, if they lose an argument, their feeling of rejection will be even stronger.

- **Be Willful.** The perfect example is the child whose mother tells him to sit down, but he is so adamant to do it his way that when we sits, in his mind he repeats to himself, "I am standing up."

- **Be Rebellious.** This is a common symptom in a person with a root of rejection. He finds it difficult to submit, and is always arguing and asking for reasons why something needs to be done.

2. Symptoms of self-rejection

This is the second part of rejection and it has to do with one's personal intimacy and self-respect, and it is reflected in the person's concept of self.

- **Low self-esteem.** This person considers himself insignificant and worthless.

- **Feeling inferior to others and insecure.** This individual is self-doubting and tries to find his confidence and security in people, things, pets or money.

- **Feelings of inadequacy.** The person fears he is unable to do things right, or that he is incapable of accomplishing anything.

- **Sadness or grief.** These are external manifestations of the wounded soul and wounded spirit, which is always sad and depressed.

- **Self-condemnation.** Such people always tear themselves down and blame themselves when anything goes wrong. They have a weak temperament, and are easily manipulated and controlled by others.

- **The inability to communicate.** It is very difficult for such a person to open his heart to others because of his inability to communicate his feelings adequately. Such people tend to be mistrusting of everyone and assume that if they open themselves up and express their feelings, they will be rejected.

- **All kinds of fears.** The individual is afraid of everything, including responsibility. He constantly worries about things that are yet to occur, and fears being alone.

- **Anxiety, worry and depression.** It is very common to see these three tendencies in a person with a root of rejection. This is due to his insecurities.

- **Negativity, doubt and loneliness.** The person who feels rejected always speaks negatively; he is pessimistic and feels lonely, even when people surround him.

- **Loss of identity.** As a result of all of the above, it is common to see people seek their identity in their work, gangs, sports, school, church or any place where they can feel accepted.

3. **Symptoms of the fear of rejection**

People, who are afraid of being rejected, tend to behave the same in any given situation.

- **People push themselves to succeed or compete**. They wish to obtain success in any area of their life so as to prove to others their worth and to gain their approval. They may go as far as trying to achieve this success dishonestly as they think that this way they can get other people's respect and admiration.

- **Independence and isolation.** Fear of rejection influences some people to isolate themselves from others, especially during adolescence or after a broken marriage.

- **The egocentric syndrome.** "Me, me, me." Many times, the person is self-centered and develops egocentric symptoms such as self-indulgence, self-righteousness, and self-justification.

- **The "my rights" attitude.** The rejected ego demands to be treated justly and correctly according to his or her standards, which are not necessarily the norm.

- **They are governed by criticism, a judgmental attitude, jealousy, envy and greed.** These five characteristics always go together and are part of a person's character when he has a root of rejection. For example: When he sees someone prosper or used by God, or when he feels threatened that someone else may take over his position, these aspects of their character are strongly demonstrated.

- **They feel pride, selfishness, haughtiness and arrogance.** This person tries to convince others he has something to really be proud of. He increases the measures of insecurity and of low self-esteem, to an unreachable level, forgetting God's warnings in His Word.

  "1Do not boast about tomorrow, for you do not know what a day may bring forth. 2Let another man praise you, and not your own mouth; another, and not your own lips." Proverbs 27.1, 2

- **Possessiveness and manipulation.** From childhood to adulthood, in marriage and outside of marriage, victims of rejection always proclaim the message "This is mine, leave it alone." People who feel rejected often console themselves with material possessions. They are jealous, manipulative, and extremely possessive.

- **Emotional immaturity.** Rejection in childhood and adolescence delays a person's emotional maturity. Such a man or woman could be 50 years old and still be emotionally immature.

- **Perfectionism**. Perfectionism can be a hereditary problem that begins when a person is rejected. He continually declares the following: "I will put up my best effort to do what is expected of me. I will please people to make them like me."

- **Interrupted sleep patterns.** Sleep is often abruptly interrupted.

Unhealthy ways to escape rejection:

- **Alcohol.** Some people drink alcohol during times of stress because they have yet to find constructive ways to escape from the pressures of life.

- **Sexual gratification.** Men, as well as women, seek sexual solace through masturbation, pornography, and other lustful acts. But sexual gratification of any kind never cancels the root of rejection.

- **Food.** Some men and women become compulsive eaters in order to compensate for the feeling of rejection. When they eat too much, rejection becomes worse because over-eating increases their weight leading to lower self-esteem, and may even give way to the spirit of gluttony.

- **Drugs.** Some people become addicted to drugs in order to ease the pain of rejection. As a result, spirits of addiction enter their lives.

- **"Popularity at any price" syndrome.** Sadly, many people desperate for acceptance and affection come to us for prayer. In their desperate attempt to find these, they submit to every type of immoral sexual activity. They twist their own sense of worth by performing certain regrettable acts, even though they hated doing these things. They did all these things in exchange for acceptance and love.

Rejection can be seen at three levels: at the root of one's being, as self-rejection and as fear of rejection. To better understand this, let us look at the following chart:

The Tree of Rejection and its Roots:

Symptoms of the Root of Rejection	Symptoms of Self-Rejection	Symptoms of the Fear of Rejection
	Low self-esteem	Competitiveness
Aggressive reactions	Inferiority	Search for success
Refusal to be consoled	Insecurity	Independence
Rejection of others	Grief, Sadness	Isolation
Emotional hardness	Self-condemnation	Egocentrism
Doubt, disbelief	Self-accusation	Selfishness, Self-justification
Aggressive attitudes	Inability to communicate	Idolatry towards oneself
Dirty language, swearing	Fear to failure	Judgment, jealousy, envy, coveting
Thoughts of vengeance	Fear of others' opinions	Self-compassion, pride, selfishness, rudeness
Argumentative	Anxiety, worry	Arrogance, manipulation, control
Foolishness	Depression, negativity	Emotional immaturity
Rebellious	Pessimism	Perfectionist
Fights	Loneliness, despair	

The fruit and roots of rejection   **The fruit depends on the level of rejection**

Note taken from the book: *Evicting Demonic Intruders* by Noel and Phyl Gibson (Ventura, C.A. Renew Books 1998)

How to be set free from rejection

The first thing a person who feels rejected needs to understand is that Jesus Christ was rejected, so that we could be accepted in Him. Jesus experienced rejection, loneliness, pain, anguish and betrayal. His own people rejected Him, because of this millions of people now receive deliverance from rejection.

"1Who has believed our report? And to whom has the arm of the Lord been revealed? 2For He shall grow up before Him as a tender plant, and as a root out of dry ground. He has no form or comeliness; and when we see him, there is no beauty that we should desire Him. 3He is despised and rejected by men, a man of sorrows and acquainted with grief. And we hid, as it were, our faces from Him; He was despised, and we did not esteem Him. 4Surely He has borne our griefs and carried our sorrows; yet we esteemed Him Stricken, smitten by God, and afflicted." Isaiah 53.1-4

"11He came to His own, and His own did not receive Him." John 1.11

We need to understand that for every sin and work of the flesh there is a corresponding demon. The book of Galatians says jealousy is a work of the flesh; however, the enemy can also send a spirit of jealousy to someone of his choosing. Lust is a work of the flesh, but there is also a spirit of lust.

What happens when we feel rejected?

For a long time we practice rebellion, perfectionism, control and manipulation. We isolate ourselves from people, become prideful, criticize and judge others. If we keep acting the same way deliberately, what we do becomes a habit first, and then it becomes a way of life. Without a doubt, this opens doors for demonic spirits to influence and oppress those of us who are in this condition.

Demons work in groups. The demon of rejection keeps an open door in our lives that attract other spirits who will come and try to influence us. Examples of such spirits are: spirits of jealousy, envy, lust, rebelliousness, pride, fear, grief, abandonment, sadness, anger, and many more.

This does not mean we have all of these demonic influences oppressing us, but how many spirits are around us depend on the level of rejection we are exposed to.

Renounce to the spirit of rejection

Every oppressed or demonically influenced person should desire with all of his or her heart to be set free from it by doing the following:

▪ They should make sure they are not harboring an unforgiving heart.

- They need to be sure they are not holding onto any sin they have yet to repent of.

- It is also crucial that they are not living in sin.

Steps to be set free from the spirit of rejection:

1. Forgive and renounce to all lack of forgiveness. Include every person who has rejected you at any stage of your life.

2. Verbally renounce all spirits of rejection, self-rejection and fear of rejection. Also, renounce any generational curse inherited through the bloodline of parents and ancestors, and order every spirit behind that curse to get out of your life.

3. Renounce to all related spirits such as: fear, jealousy, envy, lust, masturbation, pride, grief, abandonment, sadness and others.

4. Ask the Lord to fill the void left in your life with the Word of God and the Holy Spirit.

5. Meditate on Scriptures that affirm your acceptance in Christ.

As mentioned above, rejection is the enemy's master plan to destroy God's people, but where there is knowledge about this plan, the enemy can neither have dominion nor take control.

Levels of rejection vary from one person to another, but regardless of how much we have been rejected; Jesus came to destroy the works of the devil. Receive in faith what Jesus did for us and be set free and delivered from rejection. Amen!

CHAPTER

❧❧❧ 6 ❧❧❧

Guilt

G uilt is one of society's greatest problems, today. It is a consequence of the abundance of sin in the world, and it is also a problem in the church of Jesus Christ. Many believers still feel guilty for past sins and have yet to forgive themselves, or fully believe in the work that Jesus accomplished at the cross.

What is guilt?

The Greek word *"hupodikos"* means one under judgment, who is suffering the consequences or punishment for his evil actions. It is a feeling of being in a bad relationship with God.

Guilt comes from violating our conscience and it produces anxiety. It is associated with the fear of being punished for evil actions. When we deny or try to hide our guilt through rationalization, guilt is transferred from the conscious to the subconscious. One cause of panic attacks is subconscious guilt.

The Difference between Condemnation and Conviction

Condemnation is when the enemy makes us feel guilty; it comes into our mind and brings condemnation for something we did in the past, even after we ask the Lord for forgiveness.

Conviction is a sense of having done something wrong, it is revealed by the Holy Spirit, into our conscience, and it usually happens when a sin is recently committed. The Holy Spirit convinces us that we have offended God, but once we repent, God removes the feeling of wrongdoing. Condemnation comes from outside the mind and is produced by the enemy; conviction comes from within the mind, and is produced by the Holy Spirit.

"8And when He has come, He will convict the world of sin, and of righteousness, and of judgment." John 16.8

Guilt is the result of two things in our lives:

- Not forgiving ourselves.
- Not appropriating Jesus' redemptive work.

Sometimes, when people live in guilt and hear about freedom, they perceive it as a threat because guilt has already become part of their lives.

What are the characteristics of a person with a sense of guilt?

1. **Self-Punishment.** When people sin, they expect to suffer the consequences before obtaining for-giveness. When they think they have suffered enough, then they seek to be pardoned. There are people who say, "I have to suffer for this because I deserve it." But when we operate in this manner, we are insulting and denying Jesus' sacrifice on the cross of Calvary, His redemptive work is enough to cancel the need for us to suffer in order to be forgiven or accepted.

2. **Unworthiness.** The enemy sends such thoughts as: Why should God answer my prayers? Could I be worthy of God's forgiveness after all I have done? Can God use me?

   Even though we are not worthy, Christ made us worthy by His grace. We need to approach God's throne, trusting and knowing that we are able to do it by His grace.

   "10That you may walk worthy of the Lord, fully pleasing Him, being fruitful in every good work and increasing in the knowledge of God." Colossians 1.10

   "19Therefore, brethren, having boldness to enter the Holiest by the Blood of Jesus, 20by a new and living way which He consecrated for us, through the veil, that is,

His flesh, [21]and having a High Priest over the house of God...." Hebrews 10.19-21

The person who feels guilty tries to cope using compulsive behavior.

They may become addicted to drugs, alcohol, sexual adventures, materialism or any other destructive or compulsive act. This person tries to fill the void in his soul, or distract his mind with things, other than his guilt. Compulsive behavior is a way of saying: "God, I want to thank you for Christ's death, but that was not enough for me." Such people constantly strive in the flesh in order to forgive themselves.

3. **Compulsive behaviors.** The person who feels guilty tries to rise above that by taking on compulsive behaviors.

   Some of these behaviors can be:

   - Drugs
   - Alcohol
   - Sexual adventures
   - Materialism
   - Being a workaholic
   - Exercise
   - Food
   - Shopping

He tries to fill in the void in his soul with whatever he sees possible. This person tries to engage
in something that does not remind him of his
guilt. Surrendering to compulsive behaviors is
like saying: "God, I want to thank you for Christ's
death, but it is not enough." He is always trying
by human means to reach his own forgiveness.

4. **False humility.** Many people have the mistaken
   belief that the more impoverished they are, the
   more God will love them. They believe they are
   not worthy of anything and deprive themselves of
   material things. Many times they say, "I do not
   deserve this because I am not good enough." It is
   very difficult for this type of person to receive
   God's blessings.

Why is it so difficult to forgive ourselves?

Guilt is the result of not forgiving ourselves. Why?

Believing that forgiveness is based on one's deeds.
God's forgiveness is not based on our own works, but
on the redemptive work of Jesus Christ on the cross.
We receive forgiveness because of His grace.

A spirit of disbelief. We do not exercise faith in God,
if we do not know how to forgive ourselves. Disbelief
is a hindrance to forgiveness. Many people want to
feel something special when forgiven, but forgiveness
must be received in faith.

Identifying and yielding to the sense of guilt. We can live a long time with guilt and self-condemnation, believing that deliverance is impossible to achieve. Many do what they know is right, but they can't help feel guilty for everything and this opens the door to the spirit of condemnation.

Expectation of repeating the sin. We know God can forgive, but the reason many are unable to forgive themselves is because they believe they are going to keep repeating the same sin, over and over again. Christ died for our sins regardless of whether they were committed yesterday or today. He even died for every sin we may commit in the future.

What are the consequences of guilt?

1. **Guilt drains our energy and makes us physically and mentally ill.**

2. **Guilt blocks our relationship with God.** It is very difficult for someone who struggles with guilt to have an intense relationship with anyone, including God. Is there a sin that God cannot forgive? Blasphemy against the Holy Spirit is the only unforgivable sin. The blood of Christ forgives and cleanses every other sin. Some Biblical examples of believers who sinned and were forgiven by God are: Peter, who denied Jesus, and Paul who persecuted the church.

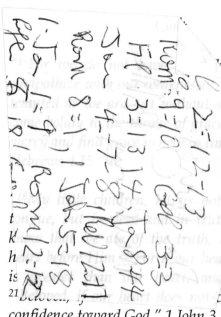

Priest who cannot ... ut was in all points ... 1. 16Let us therefore ... that we may obtain ... of need."

... love in word or in ... 1. 19And by this we ... nd shall assure our ... rts condemn us, God ... knows all things. 21Beloved, ... condemn us, we have confidence toward God." 1 John 3.18-21

How to be free of guilt

- Repent from the sin of disbelief.
- Renounce every spirit of guilt and the reasons for it.
- Confess your freedom and make the decision to receive it by faith.

What to do if the enemy accuses us and reminds us of our past.

- Confess the Word of God

> "32He who did not spare His own son, but delivered Him up for us all, how shall He not with Him also freely give us all things? 33Who shall bring a charge against God's elect? I am God who justifies. 34Who is he

who condemns? Is it Christ who died, and furthermore is also risen, who is even at the right hand of God, who also makes intercession for us?" Romans 8.32-34

- Walk in the Spirit

    "¹There is therefore now no condemnation to those who are in Christ Jesus, who do not walk according to the flesh, but according to the spirit." Romans 8.1

    "²⁵If we live in the Spirit let us also walk in the Spirit." Galatians 5.25

In conclusion, if we are born again, we need to appropriate for ourselves the redemptive work of Jesus Christ. First, we must accept God's forgiveness; and second, forgive ourselves. Remember, we need to accept this by faith.

How to be free from emotional wounds

There are many believers whom the Lord has freed from wounds, traumas and bitterness, lack of forgiveness, rejection, and guilt; and yes, they continue free for a while, but when others offend them again, they go back to being the same. We need to learn how to maintain our freedom in God. Jesus said we need offenses and hardships (*Matthew 18.1-7*). We will always be offended, wounded and hurt, but we **must** learn to live free from them.

After we are free, we must fill that void left in our hearts.

The voids should be filled with:

- The fruit of the Spirit
- The Word of God

If the void is not filled, it is easy to fall back.

Remember that to live in the Holy Spirit implies sacrifice, surrender, and discipline. We need self-discipline. If God has given you freedom and inner healing, fill yourself with the Word of God, meditate on it and live it; in this way developing the fruit of the Spirit in your heart.

We must keep in mind that healing does not replace dying to the flesh. The Lord said to deny ourselves everyday. We will be offended and hurt, but even so forgiveness must be a way of life for us if we want to continue to be free.

Six steps to continue to be free from wounds:

1. **Forgiveness must be a way of life.** Every person has to develop a permanent and genuine attitude of forgiveness in their hearts.

   "²¹Then Peter came to Him and said, "Lord, how often shall my brother sin against me, and I forgive him? Up to seven times?" ²²Jesus said to him, "I do not say to

you, up to seven times, but up to seventy times seven."
Matthew 18.21, 22

2. Let go of the offense immediately after being offended.

"26Be angry, and do not sin": do not let the sun go down on your wrath.'" Ephesians 4.26

"23Therefore if you bring your gift to the altar, and there remember that your brother has something against you, 24leave your gift there before the altar, and go your way. First be reconciled to your brother, and then come and offer your gift." Matthew 5.23, 24

"4If the spirit of the ruler rises against you, do not leave your post; for conciliation pacifies great offenses." Ecclesiastes 10.4

Why do we have to do it immediately?

- Because, otherwise, the enemy will win territory over us since we are giving him the right to do so, and that right can bring about as consequence, illnesses, poverty, binding and more.

- Because the wound can become greater. An offense causes resentment, lack of forgiveness, bitterness and eventually, hatred.

Offense ► Resentment ► Lack of Forgiveness
► Root of Bitterness ► Hatred

3. **Repent.** Just as forgiveness, repentance also has to be   a lifestyle.

What is repentance?

Repentance is to feel a deep hurt first for offending God and then also other people. Its to want to die and leave behind who we have been. It is to allow God to change us to be who He wants us to be from this moment on. It is not to cry a lot without remorse for offending God. Neither is it to try to change to avoid the consequences. It is a genuine hurt for have had caused an offense towards God or another human being.

God's Word says that to fear God is to hate evil (*Proverbs 8.13*). When you start to love and fear God, simultaneously, you will start to hate evil.

In the church today, there are many believers that do not feel enough hate for what is evil. When you fear God, you cannot support evil nor hypocrisy. The Word of God does not say to be in disagreement nor to have feelings of regret for what has happened, but rather to hate sin with all of your heart. Many people enjoy their bad habits and live in sin, and continue to do so; and this is because they have not reached the point of hating enough so as to allow God to make them free.

4. **Confess the faults.** In Greek, the word **confess** is *"exomologeo"*, which means to make known the hurts of your soul through your confession. Do not fall in the tap of the enemy to arbor all the offenses and wounds, because they start to accumulate until they explode to make the situation even worse. When does the person let go of the sin or fault? -- When he confesses it.

"⁹If we confess our sins, He is faithful and just to forgive us our sins and to cleanse us from all unrighteousness." 1 John 1.9

5. **Humility is the recognition of our condition before God.** Humility is the complete absence of pride; the voluntary submission. We need humility to forgive those who have hurt us. We also need humility to ask for forgiveness from those whom we have offended. One of the characteristics of believers is that we rarely ever ask for forgiveness. **Don't expect the other person to take the initiative to ask for forgiveness.**

6. **Known your true identity.** There are some questions we must ask ourselves. "Who am I?" "What do I see when I look in the mirror?" As man thinks of himself in his heart, so it is. Meditate on these biblical verses: *"we are your creation;"* *"God created me with a purpose."*

If we want to know who we are, we must look into the mirror of the Word. There are many people on the outside telling you who you are, but in reality, they do not know. Do not allow the opinion of others to influence your decisions nor your self-esteem.

"13When Jesus came into the region of Caesarea Philippi, He asked His disciples, saying, "Who do men say that I, the Son of Man, am?" Matthew 16.13

"10For we are His workmanship, created in Christ Jesus for good works, which God prepared beforehand that we should walk in them." Ephesians 2.10

"16Your eyes saw my substance, being yet unformed. And in Your book they all were written, the days fashioned for me, when as yet there were none of them." Psalms 139.16

"23For if anyone is a hearer of the word and not a doer, he is like a man observing his natural face in a mirror; 24for he observes himself, goes away, and immediately forgets what kind of man he was." James 1.23, 24

How to find your identity?

- Looking into the mirror of the Word.

- Asking the Holy Spirit.

This will give you security in who you are and where you are going; and it will give you the certainty that you are loved. You are not an outcast. We are a holy temple with purpose, to whom God gave the breath of life to achieve His purpose in us and in this world.

Be assured to believe and stand firm in the Divine promises of deliverance and healing in every area of your life.

Remember that this is bread for the children that live under the blessed pact of God. Amen!

CHAPTER

7

The Four Spiritual Laws

Many believers who received inner healing may still feel that they have unresolved issues. This happens because they have violated the four spiritual laws. We are the product of our actions *(Ephesians 6.1; Galatians 6.7; Matthew 7.1, 2; Romans 2.1).*

"¹Children, obey your parents in the Lord, for this is right." Ephesians 6.1

"⁷Do not be deceived: God cannot be mocked. A man reaps what he sows." Galatians 6.7

"¹Do not judge, or you too will be judged. ²For in the same way you judge others, you will be judged, and with the measure you use, it will be measured to you." Matthew 7.1

"¹You, therefore, have no excuse, you who pass judgment on someone else, for at whatever point you judge the other, you are condemning yourself, because you who pass judgment do the same things." Romans 2.1

The Four Great Biblical Laws

1. Honor thy father and thy mother.
2. Judge not and you will not be judged.

3. As a man sows, so shall he reap.
4. When we judge others, we will suffer the same thing.

Each of these spiritual laws is a principle in the Word of God. If any of these are violated, we will reap of its fruit.

A **law** always works, and anyone who applies it, whether for good or evil, will sooner or later reap of its fruit. Each of these laws warrants a detailed explanation as follows:

1. Honor thy father and thy mother.

What does "honor" mean? To honor means to obey, value, highly regard, respect, love and forgive. It also means to help our parents financially. Perhaps our parents were not the best, but that does not excuse us from the responsibility as children of God to love and honor them.

"16Honor your father and your mother, as the LORD your God has commanded you, so that you may live long and that it may go well with you in the land the LORD your God is giving you." Deuteronomy 5.16

There are sons and daughters who curse and mistreat their parents verbally and physically, and some even raise their hands against them. Such children will eventually reap the dishonoring of their parents. We cannot dishonor our parents without suffering the consequences.

How can we honor our parents?

- **Honor them emotionally.** We need to express our love for them during the difficult moments in their lives and spend time with them as often as possible. Sometimes parents go through trials and loneliness; children should support them during these difficult times.

- **Honor them verbally.** Even when parents have wrong ways of thinking, this does not give us the right to disrespect them verbally. As an authority over us, we should obey them.

  "[1]Children, obey your parents in the Lord, for this is right." Ephesians 6.1

- **Honor them financially.** When our parents reach the point when they cannot support themselves, we have the responsibility to help them financially. This pleases the Lord.

  "[2]Honor your father and mother"--which is the first commandment with a promise." Ephesians 6.2

What are the benefits of fulfilling this first law?

Things will go well with you and you will have a long life on earth. If things are not going well for you, ask yourself if you have been honoring your parents. Depending on your conscience, ask for forgiveness, then respect them, honor them, and uphold their worth.

2. **Judge not and you shall not be judged.**

    To judge is to sentence or to condemn. It also means to put yourself in the judge's seat, deciding someone's guilt or innocence.

    "37Judge not and you shall not be judged. Condemn not, and you shall not be condemned. Forgive, and you shall be forgiven." Luke 6.37

    "1Do not judge and criticize and condemn others, so that you may not be judged and criticized and condemned yourselves. 2For just as you judge and criticize and condemn others, you will be judged and criticized and condemned, and in accordance with the measure you [use to] deal out to others, it will be dealt out again to you." Matthew 7.1, 2

    Believers will have a holy and acceptable judgment. The Bible tells us:

    "4And I saw thrones, and they sat on them, and judgment was committed to them." Revelation 20.4

    When we judge, we run the risk of bringing about erroneous results for our lives and our testimonies. These risks are as follows:

Incorrect judgment: Many people judge others by their appearance without knowing what is in their heart. In Matthew 7.1-2, judgment is accompanied by envy and jealousy. The person lacking forgiveness in his heart should not only ask to be pardoned for this offense, but also for judging others.

People and groups sometimes judge organizations, nations, races, leaders, politicians, employers, spouses, pastors and many others.

Roots of bitterness and judgment: Those who expect to be rejected, betrayed, hurt, or criticized always expect something bad to happen. When it does, they say: "I knew this was going to happen." Their negative expectation becomes a self-fulfilling judgment.

How do judgmental people justify themselves?

They justify their reasons. They believe that what they are doing is correct, but this is not enough of a reason to judge.

For example, a pastor who had been freed from the habit of smoking, and now three years later he is judging another person for doing the same. Yes, smoking is not correct, but that does not give us the authority to condemn your brother or sister, and even less when you yourself had been doing the same before; on the contrary, you should feel greater compassion and have a desire to help him or her to be free from this bondage.

With comments or "constructive criticism". For example, they may comment, "That person should not be up there singing because they are of the world." This is still a judgment, whether your justification be your interest in the sanctity of the service being rendered to God.

They make an excuse before commenting. Phrases such as: "I never say anything about anyone, but…" or "I have never judged anyone and it's not that I am judging them, but…". Often, we want to alleviate the conscience before making the judgment.

3. **When we judge others, we fall under the same judgment.**

James is a good example. He was a married man who had a good relationship with his wife; and appeared to be serious and responsible. But at night, he would frequently visit bars, consuming alcohol, meeting various women and committing adultery. He really did not want to do this and he felt bad because he loved his wife and she trusted him. He would repeatedly tell himself: "I don't understand, I don't want to do this, but I can't stop." What James could not recall was that in the past, he himself would constantly judge his dad for the same behavior. His dad had been an alcoholic and a womanizer; this judgment had brought upon him the same spirit that had dominated his own father.

By judging his father, James was dishonoring him, but with time, he followed his footsteps. We see that as he judged, so was he judged. What he had so criticized in his dad, so happened to him. Praise be to God, James was prayed for, he repented and was set free. Amen!

"[1]Therefore you are inexcusable, o man, whoever you are who judge, for in whatever you judge another you condemn yourself; for you who judge practice the same things." Romans 2.1

How does one stop judging?

➤ Repent for the sin of judgment. Be specific.
➤ Confess the sin.
➤ Let go of the judgments you made against others.
➤ Bless the people you judged.

When you judge a person, you create an invisible wall.

Ask yourself if there are there things in your life that are not going according to plan? It could be that in that area, you have judged someone and you are reaping the fruit of your judgment.

4. As a man sows, so shall he reap.

What this law means, in reality is the equivalent of the worldly saying: "Don't do to others what you don't want be done to you," and I will add: "Do to others what you want for you and for yours."

"12So then, whatever you desire that others would do to and for you, even so do also to and for them, for this is (sums up) the Law and the Prophets."
Matthew 7.12

To sow is to give someone else something, be it a good deed, a gift, or something bad. To reap is to receive, or get back.

This creates a cycle in the spiritual realm: When we sow something good, we reap blessings; or the opposite, if we sow evil, cruelty or deceit, we will reap the fruit of evil. As with other laws, this one does not fail. What we live today is the direct result of what we have sown in the course of our lives.

It is essential to review what we have done or given to others, and how much love we have provided to those around us, whether we know them well or not. If you know that changes are needed in your heart in this area, make them! Your future and that of your loved ones will benefit because they also will partake of the good you do to others.

What do we sow? -- Love? -- Money? -- Time? Whatever we sow, whether it is to the spirit or the flesh, we will reap it.

"7Do not be deceived and deluded and misled; God will not allow Himself to be sneered at (scorned, disdained, or mocked by mere pretensions or professions, or by His precepts being set aside.) [He inevitably deludes himself who attempts to delude God.] For whatever a man sows, that and that only is what he will reap. 8For he who sows to his own flesh (lower nature, sensuality) will from the flesh reap decay and ruin and destruction, but he who sows to the Spirit will from the Spirit reap eternal life. 9And let us not lose heart and grow weary and faint in acting nobly and doing right, for in due time and at the appointed season we shall reap, if we do not loosen and relax our courage and faint. 10So then, as occasion and opportunity open up to us, let us do good [morally] to all people [not only being useful or profitable to them, but also doing what is for their spiritual good and advantage]. Be mindful to be a blessing, especially to those of the household of faith." Galatians 6.7-10

Often we do not reap at the same time we are sowing. It may take months and even years, but eventually harvest time comes, unless, of course, there is no repentance.

Deliverance is the Children's Bread

A desperate woman from Canaan came to Jesus seeking deliverance for her daughter, who was being tormented by a demon. Because she was a Gentile, she was not included in God's covenant with the children of Israel, but she did not allow this to stop her. When she encountered Jesus, she begged Him for help as if she were an Israelite, using words and covenant terms to which she was not entitled to: "Lord, son of David, have mercy on me." When Jesus heard the woman speak, He did not answer her right away. The disciples insisted that Jesus send her away, but Jesus calmly said two important things: *"I was not sent except to the lost sheep of the house of Israel."* Jesus was referring to the people of Israel, the only ones who were included in God's covenant. They were the only ones with legal rights to the blessings of this covenant, which included health, deliverance, salvation, protection, and provision.

The second thing that Jesus said was: *"It is not good to take the children's bread and throw it to the dogs."* What was Jesus referring to? The only ones with a right to the blessings of the covenant were the children of Israel. What was this woman asking for? She was asking for deliverance for her daughter, even though she did not have any right to those blessings because she was not from Israel. The Jews considered the Gentiles "dogs", In other words, Jesus knew that Abraham's descendants had the right to sit on God's table and the Gentiles were not permitted to do so. Some religious people do not understand this, but that is exactly what Jesus said (Matthew 15.21-28).

"21And going away from there, Jesus withdrew to the district of Tyre and Sidon. 22And behold, a woman who was a Canaanite from that district came out and, with a [loud, troublesomely urgent] cry, begged, Have mercy on me, o Lord, Son of David! My daughter is miserably and distressingly and cruelly possessed by a demon! 23But He did not answer her a word. And His disciples came and implored Him, saying, Send her away, for she is crying out after us. 24He answered, I was sent only to the lost sheep of the house of Israel. 25But she came and, kneeling, worshiped Him and kept praying, Lord, help me! 26And He answered, It is not right (proper, becoming, or fair) to take the children's bread and throw it to the little dogs. 27She said, Yes, Lord, yet even the little pups (little whelps) eat the crumbs that fall from their [young] masters' table. 28Then Jesus answered her, o woman, great is your faith! Be it done for you as you wish. And her daughter was cured from that moment." Matthew 15.21-28

The woman acknowledged the privilege and priority to receive God's blessings, but even so, she appealed to Jesus' unconditional concern to heal her possessed daughter. Jesus said to her: "It is not good to take the children's bread and throw it to the dogs." We can conclude from this that **deliverance is first, for the children of God,** and then for non-believers.

In God's plan, the gospel had to be presented first to the people of the old covenant because of the calling they received. The call for the ingathering of Israel had to precede the ingathering of the Gentiles. The woman laid hold of the blessings of the future church by faith, and in that instant her daughter was totally healed.

After this incident, Jesus went to the cross and paid for everything that had not been included in this first covenant in order to give man all that he needed. He said, **"It is finished,"** meaning, "The work is fulfilled." Now anyone who believes in Him can enjoy salvation, deliverance, forgiveness, divine provision, protection, and eternal life.

Deliverance belongs to all of us who are born again, the children of God. Jesus paid for all our sins, rebellion, generational curses, rejection and more. And so the question arises: What further deliverance could we possibly need if Jesus redeemed us from everything?

Let us remember that the Spirit of God came to live in us, but that our soul and body are still influenced by our past. For the Holy Spirit to live in fullness in us, we need to clean house. Many have made a direct or indirect pact with the enemy, and some carry generational curses in their bloodlines that must be broken. Sometimes deliverance is immediate, and at other times it is progressive.

Many believers know they are free in theory, but they have yet to take hold of the complete freedom that belongs to them. After the death and resurrection of Jesus, He raised us up with Him giving us a new life of hope. Now, everyone who wants to, can partake freely from His table and enjoy all the blessings, because He has made us His sons and daughters in faith.

Deliverance is a Mystery

There are many mysteries in the Bible, but the mystery of deliverance is one that I find people have difficulty understanding. Why are there so many pastors and ministers who do not understand the mystery of deliverance? Why are there ministers that criticize and oppose this ministry, since we all read the same Bible? The reason is simple. The ministry of casting out demons and deliverance is a **mystery** and can only be understood by revelation from the Holy Spirit.

"⁹The hypocrite with his mouth destroys his neighbor, but through knowledge the righteous will be delivered." Proverbs 11.9

If we want to see principalities and dominions of the air shattered, we need to cast out the demons here on earth. There are some who want to wage spiritual warfare in the city and in the air, without first casting the demons out of people. But when demons are cast out of people, this will affect the principalities of the air. God is raising up an army that is casting out demons all over the world.

When Jesus sent out the twelve disciples, as written in the book of Matthew, the first thing He gave them was the authority to cast out demons.

"17Then the seventy returned with joy, saying, "Lord, even the demons are subject to us in Your name." 18And He said to them, "I saw Satan fall like lighting from heaven. 19Behold, I give you the authority to trample on serpents and scorpions, and over all the power of the enemy, and nothing shall by any means hurt you. 20Nevertheless do not rejoice in this, that the spirits are subject to you, but rather rejoice because your names are written in heaven."
Luke 10.17-20

"1And when He had called His twelve disciples to Him, He gave them power over unclean spirits, to cast them out, and to heal all kinds of sickness and all kinds of diseases."
Matthew 10.1

Deliverance was a very important aspect of His ministry. If we analyze this ministry carefully, we will find a difference between Jesus' ministry and all the ministries that preceded Him – His ministry was one of deliverance, contrary to the ministries found in the Old Testament; for instance, when God called the great prophets Elijah, who prayed for rain and fire from the heavens, and Moses, who opened the Red Sea. However, none of the men of God ever cast out demons. The closest case is that of David, when he worshiped God and played the harp, the unclean spirit tormenting Saul would temporarily leave him. Christ's deliverance ministry in the New Testament separates Him from other servants of God.

The Ministry of Deliverance

The Son of God is the one who introduced deliverance. He began His ministry, by casting out demons and delivering the captives from the devil's oppression. The prophet Isaiah foretold that the Messiah would be anointed to proclaim liberty to the captives, and to open prisons to those who are bound.

"1The Spirit of the Lord God is upon me, because the Lord has anointed me to preach good tidings to the poor; He has sent me to heal the brokenhearted, to proclaim liberty to the captives, and the opening of the prison to those who are bound." Isaiah 61.1

The people had never seen these things before and exclaimed; "What new thing is this?" "With what authority and power does He cast out demons?"

"Why did these signs accompany Jesus?" -- Because He came to preach the *Kingdom of God*. This was the message of the new covenant that had never been preached before.

When the kingdom of God appears, it brings about a direct confrontation with the kingdom of darkness. Satanic powers and the power of God confront one another, the results of this confrontation is deliverance from satanic oppression.

"28But if I cast out demons by the Spirit of God, surely the kingdom of God has come upon you." Matthew 12.28

Jesus is saying that casting out demons is the most visible sign that the kingdom of God has come to a person's life.

God offers more than salvation to those who believe in Him, His desire is to bring His kingdom to us. Powerful demonic influences have been governing some areas for generations, but when the kingdom of God arrives, darkness must give way. Generational curses need to be broken in families and individual lives. Christ came to free us from curses such as poverty, witchcraft, divorce, and others.

When we receive Jesus in our heart as our Lord and Savior, the kingdom of God begins to confront the spirits from the kingdom of darkness in our life, and we receive revelation of the gospel. This is a mystery to many, and foolishness to those who are still lost.

"21In that hour Jesus rejoiced in the Spirit and said, I thank you, Father, Lord of heaven and earth, that You have

hidden these things from the wise and prudent and revealed them to babes." Luke 10.21

The disciples returned happy because they had preached the Word and signs followed them; they rejoiced because the demons were subject to the name of Jesus. In response to this, Jesus rejoiced in the Spirit and gratefully prayed and praised His Father, who had hidden these things from the wise and prudent, and revealed them to babes.

Who are these babes? The word **babe** means one who is not qualified, not specialized, not an expert, **one humble enough to receive instruction.** These are the only ones that understand: the ones that are humble and gentle to receive instruction, who don't believe themselves to be experts nor qualified for the Kingdom. To those who are simple, God reveals His mysteries, His wonders, and the work of His hands.

Why does God hide these truths from some people?

- He hides these truths because they **do not want to receive revelation,** so God prevents them from seeing them; this is to say, He reveals nothing to them because they do not want to receive it. God reveals His mysteries and His Word to those who hunger and thirst for it. The Lord does not throw pearls to swine, that is why He taught His disciples in parables, so that the Pharisees and the religious people would not understand, their hearts were hardened and could not receive the true revelation of Jesus.

"¹³Therefore I speak to them in parables, because seeing they do not see, and hearing they do not hear, nor do they understand. ¹⁴And in them the prophecy of Isaiah is fulfilled, which says: Hearing you will hear and shall not understand, and seeing you will see and not perceive; ¹⁵for the hearts of this people have grown dull. Their ears are hard of hearing, and their eyes they have closed, lest they should see with their eyes and hear with their ears, lest they should understand with their hearts and turn, so that I should heal them."
Matthew 13.13-15

- Many times God hides things from people **because of their spirits of pride and arrogance.** One way God judges the spirit of pride is through **spiritual blindness.** There are people that believe they know more than others; they have many degrees and experience, and because of it, they think they know it all. Their pride in their own abilities causes "spiritual blindness" in their lives. That is why they are unable to understand deliverance, because it is a mystery. God said to Isaiah:

"⁹Go, and tell this people: "Keep on hearing, but do not understand; keep on seeing, do not perceive.' ¹⁰Make the heart of this people dull, and their ears heavy, and shut their eyes; lest they see with their eyes, and hear

with their ears, and understand with their heart, and return and be healed." Isaiah 6.9, 10

Why did God send His prophets to Israel, if the people could not understand or hear them? God was judging their stubbornness and hardness of heart. Many people will not see the mysteries of God until they humble themselves and come as children into the presence of God.

Deliverance is Jesus' Ministry

Jesus talks about the deliverance ministry and the kingdom of God as a sign that the kingdom of God has come. In *Matthew 12.30*, Jesus says something important: *"30He who is not with me is against me, and he who does not gather with me scatters abroad."*

The church has used this verse to evangelize, asking people if they are with Jesus or against Jesus. But in context, Jesus is referring to the ministry of casting out demons.

There are Christians who believe in the ministries of preaching, teaching, healing and miracles, but when it comes to the ministry of deliverance, they do not even like to talk about it. Jesus is saying in this text, if you are with me, not only will you have to be with me to preach, heal and teach, but you will also be with me in the ministry of deliverance.

The deliverance ministry exposes everything that is hidden in the heart of man. It operates through the discernment of the Holy Spirit, more so in this ministry than in any other.

If you do not like this ministry, it may be because there is a problem in your heart. This does not mean that you have not been saved or that you won't go to heaven. But though many ministers know that the people of God need deliverance, they do not want anything to do with it. As you respond to the Word of God, you reveal what is in your heart.

Jesus always had the deliverance ministry because he was anointed by his Father to free the captives; He expects you and me to believe in the complete gift that salvation brings forth. His total package includes salvation, healing, miracles, prosperity and eternal life.

Many people do not want to preach or speak about deliverance because this is Jesus' most controversial ministry. But Jesus said: if you are not with me in this ministry, then you will be against me. **If you are with me until the end, this will be the proof: that you belief and preach under the power of the ministry of deliverance.**

If you can cast out demons, you will not have problems doing anything else for God.

Deliverance

Many believers, because of the extreme beliefs, have misunderstood the deliverance ministry. Some people see demons everywhere, and others credit everything that happens in their lives to manifestations of the flesh.

What is the difference between the works of the flesh and oppression from the enemy?

To answer this question, we must first understand what the flesh is: it is the old Adamic nature, known as the old man or the carnal nature. This describes the nature we have inherited from Adam.

The problem of original sin is universal, and people from the fallen human race, inevitably come under the power of demons. If humanity had never sinned, we would not be vulnerable to demons.

Scientists say: "When a healthy body is attacked by cancerous cells, the immune system identifies them and attacks them; as a result, these cancerous cells cannot hurt the organism." It is the same with demons. They always try to attack, but when a person is spiritually healthy his spiritual immune system identifies and attacks the demons, so that they cannot take control. However, when a person is not emotionally and spiritually healthy, he is vulnerable to demonic attack.

Flesh or demon?

The remedy to conquer the flesh is **crucifixion.** Our old man has been crucified. The Apostle Paul said he had been crucified with Jesus Christ. Throughout the Bible we are taught what to do with our old nature, that is, to deny ourselves, take up the cross and follow Christ each day.

"6Knowing this, that our old man was crucified with Him, that the body of sin might be done away with, that we should no longer be slaves of sin." Romans 6.6

"20I have been crucified with Christ; it is no longer I who live, but Christ lives in me; and the life which I now live in the flesh I live by faith in the Son of God, who loved me and gave Himself for me." Galatians 2.20

The solution to the demons

Some believers have fasted, prayed, bound, rebuked, implored, and still have not gotten results. They have crucified the flesh but they still struggle with compulsive desires that affect their minds, bodies and emotions, these eventually lead to sin.

The remedy for demons is to **cast them out,** because many people are taught that believers cannot be influenced by the devil, and that when they receive Christ they become instantly set free, they are still dragging around bondages from the past that control and oppress them.

There are also believers who are trying to crucify their desires when in fact, they are caused by demons that need to be cast out. Others try to cast out demons when it is actually a problem of the flesh.

The remedy to conquer the flesh, or the old man, is crucifixion, and the remedy to conquer demons is to cast them out

Can a believer be possessed? No, a believer cannot be possessed by demons, because the Holy Spirit lives in that person, but the Word of God says that a believer can give place to the enemy through his actions.

"27...nor give place to the devil." Ephesians 4.27

What are we saying? When a believer walks in obedience to God and does not yield to the enemy, the enemy is powerless against him. However, if the person yields terrain in which a demon can operate, that demon is given a **legal right**. He cannot possess the person, but he does have permission to operate by taking a certain area under his control. Using that foothold, he can send lustful desires, licentiousness and envy, bringing oppression and depression.

Direct and indirect pacts

Some believers may have made pacts with the enemy in their past. These include the secret vows of Free-masonry, the Rosicrucian, magic, Santeria, voodoo, transcendental meditation, yoga, and promises or vows to images or statues, which are all idolatry. If they never renounced those pacts and practices of darkness, they are giving the enemy legal rights over their lives.

Believers cannot be possessed, but they can be oppressed or influenced by unclean spirits; this when doors are opened and legal rights are granted.

To possess also means to own someone in spirit, soul and body, making that person be under the complete control of demons. This can happen to unbelievers, but oppression implies influence, not possession.

When speaking of possession, we are referring to taking ownership over someone's spirit, soul and body; it is to be completely under the control of the demons. This applies to non-believers; but the oppression implies influence upon believers. For example, the enemy temporarily influenced Peter. He was burdened with fleshly compassion and did not want Christ to suffer death on the cross. Satan was behind that spirit of compassion, trying to persuade Jesus to resist going to the cross. Peter's spiritual eyes had not yet been opened to understand the glorious works of the Lamb of God, so he reasoned using his natural instincts. After that, Satan blinded his understanding further and he denied Christ three times. It was only when Christ looked upon him with compassion that he became free of that spirit, and the Holy Spirit granted him conviction and repentance. The Bible says that he cried bitterly.

The enemy can influence and oppress the mind of a believer, and that is why the Word of God exhorts us to pray in the Spirit and not fall into temptation. Let us close the doors to the enemy in our mind and hearts!

Some signs of demonic oppression are:

1. **The person feels seduced.** Demons persuade people to do bad things. We have all experienced this. When people say, "I didn't even realize what I was doing, nor did I see the danger," this indicates that they are being seduced by evil influences. For example: if someone finds a purse with money inside and immediately hears a voice saying: "Take it, nobody will know, others would do it." In this way, the enemy cunningly persuades a person to sin.

2. **The person fasts and prays without results**. All too often, believers say, "I have prayed, fasted, rebuked, gone to counseling, seen a psychologist, tried to bind and cast out spirits. Yet something stronger than me keeps making me sin." This is a diabolic oppression. That person needs to be delivered in the name of Jesus.

3. **The person feels harassed**. Demons study your movements, and observe and detect your weaknesses. Just when you think everything is under control, in a moment of discouragement the enemy springs a trap to harass you and try to make you fall.

4. **The person feels tormented:** *"³⁴In anger his master turned him over to the jailers to be tortured, until he should pay back all he owed. ³⁵This is how my heavenly father will treat each of you unless you forgive your brother from your heart." Matthew 18.34, 35*

As we have seen in previous chapters, many believers are tormented by demons for the simple reason that they have not forgiven.

Demonic torture in a person:

➢ **Physically:** The person may suffer physical afflictions such as arthritis, ulcers, paralysis, asthma, etc. I am not saying that all of these diseases are demonic, but that sometimes they are the product of demons and the result of unforgiving.

➢ **Spiritually:** These could come in the form of an accusation to cause guilt because the person committed a sin, such as murder or abortion. A spirit of guilt may torment such a person relentlessly.

5. **The person develops compulsive desires**. No word is more specific in describing demonic activity than **"compulsive."** Usually, behind every compulsive desire there is a demon. People may say, "I have an overwhelmingly compulsive desire to smoke, drink alcohol, do drugs, have constant sex, overeat or steal." Many say: "I have tried to stop, but something is pushing me to do it and I can't stop." This is a sign of demonic influence.

6. **A sense of enslavement.** Suppose for example, you committed a sexual sin and then repented with all your heart. You know God forgave you and justified you, but you still feel an intense desire to do it again. Why? -- Because there is a demonic influence. Demons cause addictions of all sorts. People battling addictions are advised to confess their problem to a servant of God and remain under consistent spiritual supervision in order to live a full and victorious life in Christ.

7. **Physical attacks.** Demons can cause physical symptoms, such as chronic fatigue. The victims feel tired when they get up, when they go to bed, all the time. They can't read the Bible or pray because they are tired. Another example of demonic physical attacks is sleep disorders. Some people read the Bible or pray and then go to sleep; however, if they watch TV they cannot sleep. Others sleep 12 to 16 hours a day as an escape; a

spirit of depression that causes the person to avoid facing reality often causes this.

Areas affected by demons.

Let us briefly summarize Chapter One of this book. Man is composed of spirit, soul and body. The spirit is born again and the Holy Spirit lives in the believer, but the soul needs to be delivered. It is in the soul where the majority of the problems are found. The soul is divided into three parts, the will, mind and emotions. God needs to free us of the influences of the enemy.

The affected areas are:

- **The emotions**. Unclean spirits reside in the heart of man and damage the emotions with feelings such as rejection, anger, hatred, and dispute.

- **The body**. There are unclean spirits that inhabit certain parts of the body. For example, sexual spirits reside in the abdomen, eyes, and back.

  "11And there was a woman there who for eighteen years had had an infirmity caused by a spirit (a demon of sickness). She was bent completely forward and utterly unable to straighten herself up or to look upward. 12And when Jesus saw her, He called [her to Him] and said to her, Woman, you are released from your infirmity! 13Then He laid [His] hands on her, and

instantly she was made straight, and she recognized and thanked and praised God." Luke 13.11-13

- **The tongue:** Evil thoughts originate in the heart, and out of the abundance of the heart, the mouth speaks.

"34Brood of vipers! How can you, being evil, speak good things? For out of the abundance of the heart the mouth speaks. 35A good man out of the good treasure of his heart brings forth good things, and an evil man out of the evil brings forth evil things. 36But I say to you that for every idle word men may speak; they will give account of it in the day of judgment. 37For by your words you will be justified, and by your words you will be condemned." Matthew 12.34-37

Some people are always talking negatively; they criticize, murmur and complain. God exhorts us to use a language of worship and to confess His Word with our mouths.

- **Appetite.** Certain spirits affect the appetite, such as gluttony and anorexia. Slimness may be in style in most parts of the world, but many people are dying because of anorexia.

- **Sex.** The spirits of lust, adultery, homosexuality and fornication seek control over many people. These spirits do not travel alone. Sexual spirits work in gangs; they follow one behind the others.

CHAPTER
❧❧❧ 9 ❧❧❧

The Origin of Demons

If we are learning about deliverance, we also should understand the enemy, the devil and his demons, their origin, how they behave, and the way their organization operates.

The Origin of Satan

- He was created perfect in all his ways.
- He was an angel of protection and anointed.
- He was full of wisdom and beauty.

"12Son of man, take up a lamentation for the king of Tyre, and say to him, 'Thus says the Lord God: "You were the seal of perfection, full of wisdom and perfect in beauty.'"
Ezekiel 28.12

"12How you are fallen from heaven, o Lucifer, son of the morning How you are cut down to the ground, you who weakened the nations. 13For you have said in your heart: 'I will ascend into heaven, I will exalt my throne above the stars of God; I will also sit on the mount of the congregation on the farthest sides of the north; 14I will ascend above the heights of the clouds, I will be like the Most High.' 15Yet you shall be brought down to Sheol, to the lowest depths of the pit. 16Those who see you will gaze at you, and consider you, saying: 'Is this the man who

*made the earth tremble, who shook kingdoms, [17]who made
the world as a wilderness and destroyed the cities, who did
not open the house of his prisoners?'" Isaiah 14.12-17*

Satan and his fall:

- He rebelled against God.
- He exalted himself because of his beauty.
- He filled himself with iniquity through his commerce.
- He defiled the sanctuary and deceived one-third of the angels.

As a consequence of his sin, he was thrown out of heaven and his final destiny is the lake of fire.

*"[7]And when the thousand years are completed, Satan will
be released from his place of confinement, [8]And he will go
forth to deceive and seduce and lead astray the nations
which are in the four quarters of the earth--Gog and
Magog--to muster them for war; their number is like the
sand of the sea. [9]And they swarmed up over the broad plain
of the earth and encircled the fortress (camp) of God's
people (the saints) and the beloved city; but fire des-
cended from heaven and consumed them. [II Kings 1.10-12;
Ezekiel 38.2, 22.] [10]Then the devil who had led them astray
[deceiving and seducing them] was hurled into the fiery
lake of burning brimstone, where the beast and false
prophet were; and they will be tormented day and night
forever and ever (through the ages of the ages)."
Revelation 20.7-10*

When did he fall? Between *Genesis 1.1* and *1.2*.

Something happened between *Genesis 1.1* and *1.2*. The Word of God says: *"In the beginning God created the heavens and the earth."* However, in verse two, it says, *"The earth was without form, and void."*

When God creates something He does it perfectly; He never creates anything that is void.

"31Then God saw everything that He had made, and indeed it was very good. So the evening and the morning were the sixth day." Genesis 1.31

The reason the earth became void and disorganized is because something happened on earth; some theologians believe that this was when Satan's rebellion occurred.

The Names of Satan

His names reveal his character, position and activities at different stages:

- **Adversary** - He is God's rival and wants to establish his own kingdom.

- **Devil** - The Greek word *"diabolos"* means slander, one that makes others stumble. *"2For forty days in the desert, where He was tempted by the devil." Luke 4.2* "Diabolos" also means one who initiates malicious and false reports in order to hurt others.

- **The ancient serpent** - Ancient because he has existed for a long time, and serpent because of his deceptive mortal venom.

"³But [now] I am fearful, lest that even as the serpent beguiled Eve by his cunning, so your minds may be corrupted and seduced from wholehearted and sincere and pure devotion to Christ." 2 Corinthians 11.3

- **The great dragon** - A destructive beast.

"³Then another ominous sign (wonder) was seen in heaven: Behold, a huge, fiery-red dragon, with seven heads and ten horns, and seven kingly crowns (diadems) upon his heads." Revelation 12.3

- **The malignant one** - The Greek word *"poneros"* means wicked and corrupt, and implies one who looks to corrupt others.

"¹⁵I do not ask that You will take them out of the world, but that You will keep and protect them from the evil one." John 17.15

- **The destructive one** - There are two words to describe destructive: *"abadown"* in Hebrew and *"apoleia"* in Greek.

- **A liar and a murderer**

"⁴⁴You are of your father, the devil, and it is your will to practice the lusts and gratify the desires [which are characteristic] of your father. He was a murderer from

the beginning and does not stand in the truth, because there is no truth in him. When he speaks a falsehood, he speaks what is natural to him, for he is a liar [himself] and the father of lies and of all that is false." John 8.44

The Enemy and his Position

- **As prince of this world.** He governs this world, "cosmos", a corrupt system dominated by men and women who are separated from God.

- **As prince of the power of the air.** His area of operation is the atmosphere around us, which is called the second heaven.

  "2In which at one time you walked [habitually]. You were following the course and fashion of this world [were under the sway of the tendency of this present age], following the prince of the power of the air. [You were obedient to and under the control of] the [demon] spirit that still constantly works in the sons of disobedience [the careless, the rebellious, and the unbelieving, who go against the purposes of God]." Ephesians 2.2 (amplified Bible)

- **The god of this era.** A philosophical system that promotes a religious order and way of life that exalts the creature over the creator.

- **The accuser.** The Bible portrays the enemy as the accuser of the brethren, who accuses us before God day and night.

"⁹Then Satan answered the Lord, Does Job [reverently] fear God for nothing? ¹⁰Have You not put a hedge about him and his house and all that he has, on every side? You have conferred prosperity and happiness upon him in the work of his hands, and his possessions have increased in the land. ¹¹But put forth Your hand now and touch all that he has, and he will curse You to Your face." Job 1.9-11

The Demons

Theologians generally accept one of two major theories about the origin of demons.

1. The theory that they are fallen angels.

"²⁴Now when the Pharisees heard it they said: "This fellow does not cast out demons except by Beelzebub, the ruler of the demons." Matthew 12.24

"⁴¹Then He will also say to those on His left hand, 'Depart from me, you cursed, into the everlasting fire prepared for the devil and his angels." Matthew 25.41

In comparing these two texts, we conclude that if the prince of demons is the devil, then his angels are demons.

2. The theory of the pre-adamic race.

This other theory proposes that demons are spirits of a race that existed before the creation of Adam.

They were destroyed when Satan fell because they followed him.

"4For if God did not spare the angels who sinned, but cast them down to hell and delivered them into chains of darkness, to be reserved for judgment..."2 Peter 2.4

➢ The fallen angels were held in prisons of darkness.

➢ God created a perfect earth and inhabited it with living beings.

➢ Lucifer was the governor of this earth and all creation.

➢ In their rebellion, these beings were destroyed.

➢ The spirits of these beings are now the demons whose final destination is the lake of fire.

➢ They look for bodies to inhabit in order to manifest themselves.

➢ This could explain the theory of the extinction of the dinosaurs and other creatures.

These are the two theory that theological schools affirm.

Descriptions of Demons

"33Now in the synagogue there was a man who was possessed by the foul spirit of a demon; and he cried out with a loud (deep, terrible) cry, 34Ah, let us alone! What have You to do with us [What have we in common], Jesus of Nazareth? Have You come to destroy us? I know Who You are--the Holy One of God!" Luke 4.33, 34

"30Jesus then asked him, What is your name? And he answered, Legion; for many demons had entered him." Luke 8.30

Some descriptions of demons, according to the Bible are:

➢ **They have personalities.** They have names, emotions, will and they can speak.

➢ **They are spirits.** They are evil, unclean spirits; named according to their manifestations, such as *a deaf and mute spirit (Mark 9.17-25).*

➢ **They cause oppression.** There are different levels of demonic control: depression, oppression, obsession and possession.

➢ **Demonic possession.** *(Mark 5.1-20)* It is a supernatural power that can cause certain manifestations in the victim. The person who is possessed does and says strange things, using her voice or a different one, and manifests a personality totally different that who he really is.

How did Jesus deal with demons?

There are five important points in these verses that illustrate how Jesus dealt with demons. (*Mark 1.22-39*)

1. Jesus dealt with the demon and not with the man.

2. Jesus expelled the demon from the man and not the man from the synagogue.

3. Jesus was not ashamed of interruptions because this was His ministry.

4. It is reasonable to assume that the man was a member of the synagogue, but that no one knew he needed deliverance.

5. It was such a dramatic confrontation that Jesus' fame and authority spread throughout the region.

Levels of Spiritual Warfare

There are three levels of spiritual warfare.

1. The Earthly/Personal Level

On this level, demons are cast out of individuals. You cannot do effective warfare against principalities of the air and strongholds of darkness, until demons are cast out of people here on earth, first.

2. The Territorial / Strategic Level

This is a battle against territorial spirits. They are authorized by man himself with his actions, giving way for the enemy to reign over specific geo-political and geographical areas such as nations, ethnic groups, cities, churches and families.

3. The Philosophical Level

This is a battle against spirits of false beliefs and philosophies that divide and hinder the growth of Christ's church.

The purpose of spiritual warfare on these three levels is:

- To deliver people so they can fulfill God's purpose effectively.

- To deliver people so they can serve God in fullness.

CHAPTER

৵৵৵ 10 *৵৵৵*

The Five Spirits of the Enemy that Attack the Church

I t is essential to examine five of the most persistent spirits that attack the church in our times. All
five are real and have caused misery in many
congregations today. We may ask, why did this happen in such a church? We need to know that we live
in a continual war, that we do not wrestle against
flesh and blood but against that enemy of God and
man, Satan, the ancient serpent.

Often, these five spirits manifest themselves through
people within the same church, yet many do not
realize the enemy is using them; others know, but do
not seek help.

1. The spirit of Jezebel.

*"But there was no one like Ahab who sold himself to do
wickedness in the sight of the Lord, because Jezebel his
wife stirred him up." 1 Kings 21.25*

Ahab was a king of Israel who disobeyed
Jehovah's law by marrying Jezebel, the daughter
of the king of Sidon in Phoenicia. Jezebel used her
power as queen to promote the worship of the
false gods Baal and Ashtoreth. The latter was the
goddess Asherah, who the Phoenicians called the

queen of heaven. Baal was the god of the storm who required human sacrifices; this was satanic worship. Ahab allowed idolatry in Israel by allowing his wife to dominate the people, and establish pagan worship, and the sacrifice of children. Ahab represents a man who is of weak spiritual character, both at home and in the church.

His flaws helped destroy Israel's priesthood. He was a passive man, and because he disobeyed the law of God, his wife Jezebel took over, dominating to the extent that she was able to influence most of the Hebrew nation to bow down and worship Baal. Only 7,000 people did not bow down before this false god.

Who was Jezebel?

She was King Ahab's controlling and manipulative wife *(1 Kings 18:14-19)*. In today's society, the spirit of Jezebel is identified as a source of obsessive sensuality, a worshiper of the occult, witchcraft, and a seeker for equality of rights for men and women alike.

Jezebel means without cohabitation; i.e., this spirit has no interest in others. She is not a team player. She is self-sufficient, and controls minds and situations under the influence of satanic spirits. She likes to monopolize and is arrogant. Through sex, she seduces and controls, not only her husband

but also her lovers. She disdains masculine authority, and is characterized by dominating and controlling her husband instead of submitting to his
headship. Simply put, she refuses to cohabit or
live with anyone unless she can control and have
dominion over the person.If she cannot accomplish this, she changes her tactics and secretly
instigates her husband to do evil, all the while
hiding behind him.

We see this spirit in the wife of King Herod, who
asked her daughter to dance in front of her husband in order to seduce him with sexual movements, and thereby to accomplish her plan to kill
God's prophet, John the Baptist.

This spirit moves in three areas:

> **The human being**. It operates in the indi-
vidual, be it man or woman. It attacks both
genders, but has greater tendency towards the
female, who generally lets herself be dominated by jealousy. It can be insecure, con-
ceited, controlling and domineering. It uses
sex because as we have seen, its greatest
strength is that of control. We can find it in
women who are bitter towards men, that
publicly humiliate them, and control them
with threats in their sexual lives. The main
objective is to control and dominate.

➤ **The church.** This spirit infiltrates the church and tries to control God's servants or to cause them to sin. It also operates in the church as a spirit of seduction and fornication. It hates the prophetic spirit and resists the fire of the Holy Spirit represented by Elijah, a figure of those servants of God who will be filled with glorious manifestations of His power in the end times.

➤ **The nation.** Jezebel operates as a principality over a nation, taking control and bringing its inhabitants into bondage. This took place in the nation of Israel when Acab allowed Jezebel to dominate the country through satanic control and idolatry.

Today the battle has intensified as this spirit uses the media as a means to operate in nations. This spirit functions unhindered in spectacles, entertainment, fashion and New Age activities. It infiltrates pornography, advertising, erotic magazines and adult videos, seducing many souls in secret, including hundreds of pastors and religious leaders.

Under the influence of this spirit, abortions have multiplied by the thousands, which is comparable to the number of child sacrifices to Baal. Jezebel also commanded that the prophets of the living God be decapitated. This has happened in Colombia, Cuba, and even in the United States.

What Jezebel Hates

- Repentance
- A humble heart
- The prophetic word of fire
- Submission
- Fasting and intercession

Its hate is against God himself and His chosen ones.

What are the characteristics of a person operating under the influence of this spirit?

Her victims often boast of revelations they have received, seeking to exalt the ego. *"²Let another man praise you, and not your own mouth; a stranger, and not your own lips." Proverbs 27:2* They are usually on the lookout for recognition. They strive desperately to be mentioned from the pulpit by church leaders, and are offended and resentful when leaders decide not to mention their names.

They try to get close to leaders through flattery and compliments, or wait expectantly to hear great prophecies about themselves that would elevate them to a position of grandeur before others. Nothing is wrong with giving compliments if a person has the correct motivation. But these people may say, "Nobody has served in this church like you do; too bad the pastor does not like and understand you."

They rarely want to be in authority, but prefer to be the **"power behind the throne."**

This spirit operates in women who say publicly, "I will submit to my husband," but dominate and control, doing what they want behind their backs.

This spirit attracts the weakest members of the church, enslaving them with flattery or false prophecies. They, in turn, look for people who are rebellious, or those who have been hurt and resist authority. This spirit knows how to manipulate the emotions. It uses its spiritual influence to spread gossip, unhappiness and division.

"16These six things the Lord hates, indeed, seven are an abomination to Him: 17A proud look [the spirit that makes one overestimate himself and underestimate others], a lying tongue, and hands that shed innocent blood, 18A heart that manufactures wicked thoughts and plans, feet that are swift in running to evil, 19A false witness who breathes out lies [even under oath], and he who sows discord among his brethren."
Proverbs 6:16-19

This spirit often tries to persuade couples to get married and then controls them with false prophesy and phrases such as: "God told me to tell you…"

Who are the potential targets of this spirit in a church?

- Pastors, evangelists, leaders with influence, worship leaders and intercessors.

- The spirit of Jezebel will try to destroy any church in revival, with the revealed Word of God, and a fresh and continuous anointing of the Holy Spirit.

- It uses children as tools to manipulate others and even manipulates children.

How to Keep Yourself from the Jezebel Spirit

The best defense is repentance and deliverance; to live with a clean heart. Genuine repentance produces divine intervention and the renewal of the presence of God in the lives of those in need.

What attitude should you have toward people influenced by this spirit?

Fight against the spirit, not against the person. Always be ready to remain free from the seduction of this terribly oppressive spirit.

2. The Spirit of Absalom

This is the spirit of treason, and it may operate in the hearts of leaders of the church.

Who was Absalom? *(2 Samuel 15.1-6)* He was a son of David who betrayed him by leading Israel into a rebellion against him in order to take over his throne and power.

This spirit operates through leaders and people who are unhappy and offended, spiritual leaders who betray the authority God has placed upon them in the congregation. This person seeks others who will back their agendas, which are usually contrary to the vision of the pastor and the church.

The spirit of Absalom often leads its followers out of the church, causing division and bringing chaos.

- This spirit, like Jezebel, likes attention and is consumed with the desire to control.

- It is independent and likes to promote itself. Even though Absalom feigned interest in the problems of the people, his true motivation was to cross his father's authority and to exalt himself *(2 Samuel 15.1-13)*.

What causes the spirit of Absalom to manifest?

- **Personal ambition.** Unhappy leaders want to be first and to promote their own agendas before that of their local churches.

  Absalom stole the hearts of people with flattery and praise. This spirit speaks to people in a way so as to start admiring it, that way causing a proud spirit that deceives the remaining "Absaloms", thinking they are more spiritual than the pastor. Then, the spirit of competition takes control; then later plants division and attracts a group of followers who have been fed by a sprit of criticism. Many times, they leave there and start other churches with their fruit of division without the presence of God.

- **An unresolved offense.** Minor offenses can become a fortress in the heart and mind of man (*2 Samuel 13.22-39*).

  Absalom had lack of forgiveness against his brother Amnon, who raped his sister Tamar. When his sister told him that Amnon had raped her, the Bible says:

  "²²And Absalom spoke to his brother Amnon neither good nor bad. For Absalom hated Amnon, because he had forced his sister Tamar."
  2 Samuel 13.22

Time passed, but he never forgave. This developed into bitterness and hate, until he finally killed his brother.

"27But Absalom urged him; so he let Amnon and all the king's sons go with him. 28Now Absalom had commanded his servants, saying, "Watch now, when Amnon's heart is merry with wine, and when I say to you, 'Strike Amnon!' then kill him..."
2 Samuel 13.27-28

Who are the targets of this spirit?

Absalom targets elders, deacons, members of boards of directors of the church, and leaders from different departments. Those influenced by Absalom spirits may serve for a while, but suddenly stop cooperating with the pastor.

Absalom in the church

We have discussed how unresolved offenses lead to sin. They can also open doors of deception from the spirit of Absalom. This spirit does not have to physically kill a person; it can do so spiritually by maligning him or her, and ruining their testimonies.

A good illustration is that of a pastor that took over a church in California. This church had been founded due to a division and thus, the presence of God was not there. The pastor went and asked the previous pastor for forgiveness and the presence of God the started to be felt. The church had initiated with division at its root.

What was the end of Absalom? He was hung, while David's throne was restored.

"8For the battle spread over the face of all the country, and the forest devoured more men that day than did the sword." 2 Samuel 18.8

Keep your minds free of this spirit. Be on guard in the areas where this spirit operates: personal ambition, unresolved offenses, etc.

What will the end be for a person who allows this spirit to influence him? The end will be sickness, death and destruction. Do not allow lack of forgiveness to fester in your heart because this will lead to bitterness and hatred, and eventually the enemy will destroy you.

3. A Pharisaic Spirit

This spirit is filled with deadly hostility. It killed Abel, crucified Jesus, stoned Stephen, and tried to destroy Paul. By nature, the Pharisaic spirit hates grace and loves legalism. Legalism is a spirit that needs to be cast out. The Pharisaic spirit wars against true worship and our relationship with

God. Cain got mad when God accepted Abel's offering and not his.

How did Jesus deal with the legalists?

- He did not mince words, calling them what they were:

  "44You are of your father the devil, and the desires of your father you want to do. He was a murderer from the beginning, and does not stand in the truth, because there is no truth in him. When he speaks a lie, he speaks from his own resources, for he is a liar and the father of it." John 8.44

- He called them sons of the devil.
- He called them whitewashed tombs.

How do victims of this spirit operate in the church?

- They love to be praised.

- They are concerned with position and honor in the church.

- They insist on governing people with their own laws and traditions.

- The religious people of the church consider themselves super-spiritual, refusing correction because they think they know it all.

- They do not enter the kingdom of heaven, nor do they permit others to do so.

- They have a strong spirit of criticism.

  "13But woe to you, scribes and Pharisees, hypocrites! For you shut up the kingdom of heaven against men; for you neither go in yourselves, nor do you allow those who are entering to go in." Matthew 23.13

- During the service, they are more interested in complying with time limitations than with God's presence.

- They do not bear fruit for God, but live for appearances.

- They place their beliefs and traditions before the Word of God.

4. The spirit of witchcraft or enchantment

This spirit controls through fear and men's traditions. It is closely related to the spirit of Jezebel. The goal of this spirit is to subject and destroy teachings of the Bible, and subsequently, Christian life. The spirit of witchcraft uses force, and at times, emotional power to manipulate others.

"19Now the works of the flesh are evident, which are: adultery, fornication, uncleanness, lewdness, 20idolatry, sorcery, hatred, contentions, jealousies, outbursts of wrath, selfish ambitions, dissension, heresies, 21envy, murders, drunkenness, revelries, and the like; of which I tell you beforehand, just as I also told you in the past, that those who practice such things will not inherit the kingdom of God." Galatians 5.19-21

Examples:

- Manipulating, controlling prayers.

- Using fear to get people to serve and not leave the church.

- Condemning messages to cause others to feel bad.

- Sowing seeds of division among the people of God.

Everything we do to control and manipulate, will be a stumbling block in the future.

What happens when a person manipulates others? Those who are manipulated become resentful and bitter. People believe they are gaining position through manipulation and control. This is a castle built on sand; when they least expect it, their castle collapses.

5. A lukewarm spirit

The lukewarm spirit operates in believers who are neither cold nor hot.

How does a person know when this spirit is operating?

- Their love for the Lord is lost or diminished.

- They lose their hunger for the things of God, the Word, prayer, and church.

- They become insensitive to the presence of God.

- They become insensitive to the needs of God's people.

- Their prayer life becomes routine.

Believers who live with these situations are vulnerable to the enemy and can be used by him at any moment. Ask the Lord for forgiveness and return to your first love of which Christ spoke, so you may be pleasing to Him.

Every church should be watchful through intercession, to prevent any of these five spirits to successfully attack them, or use people to destroy their ministries. To conquer these spirits, pray and be watchful, using the spiritual armor that God provided, which is mighty for the destruction of strongholds. Amen!

Open Doors,
an Entrance
for Demons

Demons enter through open doors in people's lives. They cannot enter or influence a person, if they have not been given a legal right to do so. Demons choose the weakest moment, and place, to invade a person.

"27...nor give place to the devil." Ephesians 4.27

Let us look at some of the open doors through which we give rights to demons to enter and influence us by bringing oppression into our lives.

1. Generational curses

Familiar spirits bring curses that are transmitted from generation to generation. These spirits are conveyed like an inheritance to the next generation.

"6And the LORD passed before him and proclaimed, "The LORD, the LORD God, merciful and gracious, longsuffering, and abounding in goodness and truth, 7keeping mercy for thousands, forgiving iniquity and transgression and sin, by no means clearing the guilty, visiting the iniquity of the fathers upon the children and the children's children to the third and the fourth generation." Exodus 34.6, 7

Generational curses manifest themselves in different forms:

- **Mental and Emotional Illness**

  This may include depression, confusion and frustration. It is not uncommon to hear people in pastoral counseling say: "My mother was always depressed and I am suffering from the same depression" (spiritual inheritance).

- **Chronic Illnesses**

  These include all types of diseases, such as cancer, diabetes, high blood pressure, asthma, arthritis, and others.

  "21The Lord will make the plague cling to you until He has consumed you from the land which you are going to posses. 22The Lord will strike you with consumption, with fever, with inflammation, with severe burning fever, with the sword, with scorching, and with mildew; they shall pursue you until you perish." Deuteronomy 28.21-22

- **Family Disintegration**

  This includes divorce, adultery, fornication, homosexuality, infertility, drug addiction, and alcoholism.

  "41You shall beget sons and daughters, but they shall not be yours; for they shall go into captivity." Deuteronomy 28.41

- **Poverty**

  Deuteronomy 28.17-29. Some people never seem able to prosper economically, living in continuous poverty. If there is any indication of this in your life, it is a sign of a generational curse in operation.

2. **Intentional sin**

   Believers sin against God by omission or by commission. Sin by omission is when we are not aware of the sin, or do not realize that what we are doing is a sin. To sin by commission is when we willfully sin, knowing it offends the Lord.

   For every voluntary sin, there is a demon that oppresses. Regularly committing the same sin opens doors to unclean spirits by giving them legal rights.

   An example of this is anger. We know that anger is an emotion and the Word of God tells us not to give way to it.

   "26Be angry, and do not sin, do not let the sun go down on your wrath, 27nor give place to the devil."
   Ephesians 4.26, 27

   The Bible also calls anger a work of the flesh. What happens if a person allows anger to turn into rage and lets the sun go down without forgiving the person who provoked the anger? This opens a door to a spirit of anger. In short, conscious sin opens doors to demons.

3. Trauma or strong emotional experiences

When trauma impacts a person's life, necessary measures must be taken in a timely manner; otherwise, it may open the door for the enemy to oppress and obsess or even posses the person.

Take the case of a little girl who was abused by another woman, when she was ten years old. When this little girl became an adult, she became a lesbian. She wanted to be with other women even though she knew it was a sin; it was a compulsive act that she could not control. The abuse opened a door that influenced her life with a spirit of lesbianism.

People who are sexually abused have two tendencies: the sex becomes uncontrollable or compulsive; or they become frigid and considers sex a repugnant act.

But we have good news: Jesus Christ came to undue the acts of the devil.

"8He who sins is of the devil, for the devil has sinned from the beginning. For this purpose the Son of God

was manifested, that He might destroy the works of the devil." 1 John 3.8

We have observed that most of the deliverances done in our church deal with childhood events which opened doors to demons. Without a doubt, we realize that this is the most vulnerable period in a person's life.

Christian parents need to understand their responsibility to protect their children. They also need to know how to free them from demonic oppression. When ministering, the first question we ask is: "How was your relationship with your parents?' This question is very important in the deliverance ministry.

4. The occult, witchcraft and false religions

The principal cause of occultism and witchcraft is idolatry. God clearly says that he hates idolatry of any kind. All forms of worship to other gods opens doors to the occult, and to witchcraft, these are ways of yielding to demons. Anyone who visits a witch is making a pact with the enemy, directly or indirectly, and this pact must be broken for the person to be set totally free. This is true even after a person receives Christ as Lord and Savior. We need to close those doors and cancel all legal rights the enemy has in the life of that person.

"3You shall have no other gods before me. 4You shall not make for yourself a carved image - any likeness of anything that is in heaven above, or that is in the earth beneath, or that is in the water under the earth;5 you shall not bow down to them nor serve them. For I, the Lord your God, am a jealous God, visiting the iniquity of the fathers upon the children to the third and fourth generations of those who hate me." Exodus 20.3-5

5. Rejection

When parents show favoritism or unequal treatment among siblings, a door opens to the enemy. Negative influences can cause rejection in the womb. Such rejection occurs when mothers hate their unborn children, either because they are unmarried, the pregnancy was the product of adultery, or the father is irresponsible.

Rejection is also a result of broken homes where there is fighting, jealousy, bitter parents, parents with no time for their children, etc. This is fertile terrain for demonic presence and activities.

"16For where envy and self-seeking exist, confusion and every evil things are there." James 3.16

6. The laying on of hands

"22Do not lay hands on anyone hastily..."
1 Timothy 5.22

When a person lays hands on another, the law of contact and transmission comes into operation. Through this law, the power of God or the power of the enemy or unclean spirits can be transferred. Since unclean spirits can be transferred from one person to another, extreme care should be taken when allowing another person to lay hands on you. Make sure that he or she is walking in integrity and holiness, regardless of whether it is a man or a woman, a leader or minister.

Absalom transferred a spirit of rebellion to the people of Israel through seduction.

A false teacher can transmit an evil spirit to another person through his false teachings. Negative, as well as positive spirits can be transmitted.

For example, Moses and Elijah transferred anointing and wisdom to Joshua and Elisha respectively, through the laying on of hands.

7. **Idle words**

The Word of God teaches that the power of life and death are in the tongue. Sometimes we curse with our mouth, giving place to unclean spirits. This is called a self-imposed curse. We use expressions such as, "I am always sick," or "My children are stupid and clumsy," or "I want to die." These spoken words impose curses and open doors to the enemy.

"³⁶But I say to you that for every idle word men may speak, they will give account of it in the day of judgment. ³⁷For by your words you will be justified, and by your words you will be condemned."
Matthew 12.36, 37

8. Soul ties

The wrong relationships --with unbelievers, fraudulent businesses, secret adulterous relationships or fornication --open doors to the enemy. Manipulation and control, or any secret relationship, opens doors to the enemy.

9. Books, videos and music

Many books, movies and music are consecrated to the devil before being distributed. As a result, anyone who listens to that type of music watches those movies or reads those books, opens doors to demons. Many rock groups make pacts with the enemy as a means of trying to succeed in their careers. They make these pacts by consecrating and dedicating their work to Satan.

10. Mental control

Some individuals allow others to hypnotize or control them mentally. Others practice telepathy or Silva Mind Control to gain psychic powers. Because the mind becomes passive, this sort of activity offers a wide open door to unclean spirits.

The enemy will not enter or influence a person unless given legal rights. The will yields the right and terrain and opens doors to demonic influence.

It is one's will power that gives authority to the enemy and opens doors through which spirits manifest their influence. The solution is to live a pure and holy life, as God has called us to live. Then the enemy cannot gain access.

CHAPTER

~~~ 12 ~~~

Breaking Curses

Generational curses are real. Unfortunately, many believers, even some evangelical ministries, do not believe that curses exist. The Word of God tells us clearly that God will punish those who do not obey His Word.

"6You shall not bow down to them nor serve them. For I, the Lord your God, am a jealous God, visiting the iniquity of the fathers upon the children to the third and fourth generations of those who hate me." Exodus 20.5

"6And the Lord passed before him and proclaimed, "The Lord God, merciful and gracious, longsuffering, and abounding in goodness and truth, 7keeping mercy for thousands, forgiving iniquity and transgression and sin, by no means clearing the guilty, visiting the iniquity of the fathers upon the children and the children's children to the third and the fourth generation." Exodus 34.6, 7

A good illustration is the story of a missionary who for many years molested his own daughter; as a consequence, he lost both his marriage and his ministry. The incest was a generational curse, because it also operated in his father and grandfather.

Redeemed from the Curse

Some people continually fail. They go through divorces, family rupture, and other unhappy events. How is it possible for a believer to continue to drag around curses? The Word of God teaches that Jesus Christ has redeemed us from the curse of the law.

"13Christ has redeemed us from the curse of the law, having become a curse for us (for it is written, "Cursed is everyone who hangs on a tree.'" Galatians 3.13

Since Jesus has redeemed us, how can a believer continue to walk and live under a curse?

"Redeem" means to buy back, to pay the debt in full. In order to understand redemption, we need to understand that it is legally ours because Jesus gave it to us, and we must appropriate the gift. In other words, we must experience it. Many believers know that Jesus legally paid for all their sins, rebellion, curses, sickness and poverty. But they have not appropriated what Jesus did in its totality.

This does not happen automatically. Believers must appropriate what was done on the cross by faith. The curse of the law includes poverty, sin, sickness, sorrow, bondage, and more. Jesus paid for all of these.

Let us take sickness as an example. The Word of God teaches that Jesus' wounds heals and redeems us from sickness. If Jesus redeems from sickness, why are there so many sick believers? The reason is that they have not appropriated and experienced their healing. Legally, Jesus accomplished it all, but many believers are still sick because they still need to take hold of what Jesus did, by faith.

The point is not to minimize what Jesus did. On the contrary, Jesus' works were perfect and He redeemed us from all curses. But we must go to the cross in faith and fight for our healing, deliverance, and all of His promises. We go to the cross to break every curse in our lives and to receive all His blessings in the name of Jesus Christ.

With this in mind, another question arises. Can a believer be under a curse?

What is a curse?

A curse is the price God established for iniquity in the lives of people and their descendants. It manifests the errors and sins of our ancestors. People often say, "My father used to do the same things I do."

How does it pass from generation to generation?

The law of inheritance is the means by which curses are set into motion. It is not pleasant to speak about this, but it needs to be brought out into the open. Good things are inherited as well. In the same manner that blessings are passed on, curses are also passed on.

The son of Noah, Ham, is an example. His sin was to see the nudity of his father and to lust over him. Sodom and Gomorrah came about as a result of that sin.

Abraham and his son Isaac are another good example. When Abraham and his wife Sarah left their land to go to Canaan, he lied and said Sarah was his sister, he did this because she was very beautiful and he was afraid the king would kill him and take Sarah for his wife. Years later, his son Isaac did the same thing with his own wife.

"¹And Abraham journeyed from there to the South, and dwelt between Kadesh and Shur, and stayed in Gerar. ²Now Abraham said of Sarah his wife, "She is my sister." And Abimelech, king of Gerar sent and took Sarah." Genesis 20.1, 2

How are blessings transmitted?

"⁶Therefore I remind you to stir up the gift of God which is in you through the laying on of my hands. ⁷For God has not given us a spirit of fear, but of power and love and a sound mind." 2 Timothy 1.6, 7

Timothy received faith from his grandmother Lois. The kind of faith we develop will be our children's inheritance. This is God's law in operation. We can choose life or death, curses or blessings.

"¹⁹I call heaven and earth as witnesses today against you, that I have set before you life and death, blessing and cursing; therefore choose life, that both you and your descendants may live." Deuteronomy 30.19

Signs and indications of curses:

➤ **Mental and emotional disturbances**

The two key words are confusion and depression. These symptoms almost always have roots in the occult. Most people who practice witchcraft or the occult, end up with dementia, depression, fear and more.

"³⁴So you shall be driven mad because of the sight which your eyes see." Deuteronomy 28.34

➤ **Chronic illness**

A chronic illness is one that has afflicted or killed many members of a family for generations. Doctors call these diseases genetic or hereditary. These include diabetes, high blood pressure, heart disease, asthma, cancer, and arthritis, to name a few.

"²¹The LORD will make the plague cling to you until He has consumed you from the land which you are

going to possess. ²²The LORD will strike you with consumption, with fever, with inflammation, with severe burning fever, with the sword, with scorching, and with mildew; they shall pursue you until you perish."
Deuteronomy 28.21, 22

A pastor diagnosed with hemochromatosis, a blood disease that produces too much iron and it hides in vital organs such as the liver or heart, renounced this inheritance from his father and was set free of the disease.

We have seen cases of diabetics who lost their parents to that disease, renounced it, broke the curse and were delivered. This can be done with any type of disease - blindness, myopia, cancer, allergies, and all others.

➤ Infertility

This includes the inability to conceive, a tendency to miscarry, menstrual irregularity, cysts, tumors and abortions.

"¹⁸Cursed shall be the fruit of your body and the produce of your land, the increase of your cattle and the offspring of your flocks." Deuteronomy 28.18

➤ Disintegration of the family

Many parents have suffered from the curse of family disintegration. They have seen their sons and daughters dedicated to drug use, sex, music, all forms of the occult, and end up divorced, widowed, or as unwed mothers.

"28Blessed shall be the fruit of your body, the produce of your ground and the increase of your herds, the increase of your cattle and the offspring of your flocks." Deuteronomy 28.4

➤ Poverty or continuous economic insufficiency

When this curse operates, no matter how much money people make, they always face financial difficulty, and never see prosperity. Money goes through their hands like water.

"47Because you did not serve the Lord your God with joy and gladness of heart, for the abundance of everything, 48therefore you shall serve your enemies, whom the Lord will send against you, in hunger, in thirst, in nakedness, and in need of everything; and he will put a yoke of iron on your neck until He has destroyed you." Deuteronomy 28.47, 48

➤ Violent or unnatural accidents

This describes the person who is prone to accidents, including unusual situations such as: a surgeon making a mistake at the operating table, or someone swallowing a fish bone. We are referring to that which is not normal or naturally occurring.

> **A sequence of suicides, premature or unnatural deaths**

People affected by this curse frequently experience strong premonitions. We are talking about a spiritual reality, an invisible enemy who needs to be destroyed.

A woman who had been sick all her life renounced this curse and was set free. How are these curses carried out? An unclean spirit causes these things to happen, and spreads them through other people.

"21However, this kind does not go out except by prayer and fasting." Matthew 17.21

> **Self-Imposed Curses**

Self-imposed curses are spoken with our own mouths and words.

"36But I say to you that for every idle word men may speak, they will give account of it in the day of judgment. 37For by your words you will be justified, and by your words you will be condemned."
Matthew 12.36, 37

"21Death and life are in the power of the tongue. And those who love it will eat its fruit." Proverbs 18.21

People should take three steps in order to be separated from the bondage of negative confessions.

1. Repent for confessing bad things.
2. Revoke and cancel those spoken words.
3. Replace them with the right confession.

What are the causes for generational curses?

"²Like a flitting sparrow, like a flying swallow, so a curse without a cause shall not alight." Proverbs 26.2

Some causes for generational curses are:

1. **Idolatry:** What is idolatry? It is to have, and to acknowledge another god before the Lord, to make a representation of it, and worship it. God punishes and judges idolatry. Many people are misled by idols, believing they are worshiping God. Others do it because it is a family tradition, and still others because of ignorance. There are also those who, even though they know the truth, do not want to accept the true God.

   "²⁰For since the creation of the world His invisible attributes are clearly seen, being understood by the things that are made, even His eternal power and Godhead, so that they are without excuse." Romans 1.20

2. **The occult:** The occult is that which is hidden. Occult practices have always fascinated the fallen

man. The three greatest aspirations of the natural man are the desire for knowledge, the longing for power, and the search for solutions to his needs.

There are two sources of knowledge and power -- the power of God and the power of the enemy. There are diverse sources -- natural and super- natural, legitimate and illegitimate. Curses also come from practicing the occult.

"10There shall not be found among you anyone who makes his son or his daughter pass through the fire, or one who practices witchcraft, or a soothsayer, 11or one who interprets omens, or a sorcerer, or one who conjures spells, or a medium, or a spiritist, or one who call up the dead. 13For all that do these things are an abomination to the Lord, and because of these abominations the Lord your God drives them out from before you. You shall be blameless before the Lord your God." Deuteronomy 18.10-13

3. **All forms of illicit or unnatural sex:** Homo-sexuals, lesbians, sex with animals, adultery, forni-cation, incest, and everything illicit and illegal before the eyes of the Lord, will bring a curse *(Leviticus 18.1-25).*

4. **Not honoring or respecting parents:** Today, there are many sons and daughters who do not do well in life because they do not honor and respect their parents.

"Children, obey your parents in the Lord, for this is right. Honor your father and mother, which is the first commandment with promise, that it may be well with you and you may live long on the earth."
Ephesians 6.1-3

5. **To curse that which God has blessed:** To curse means to speak badly about something or someone. When people speak negatively about a child of God, or something that the Lord has blessed, that curse will backfire on the one who is speaking evil. Every individual over whom God pronounces a blessing will automatically be exposed to hatred and opposition from the enemy.

   "9He bows down, he lies down as a lion; and as a lion, who shall rouse him?' "Blessed is he who blesses you, and cursed is he who curses you." Numbers 24.9

   "1Now the Lord said to Abram: Get out of your country, from your family and from your father's house, to a land that I will show you. 2I will make you a great nation; I will bless you and make your name great, and you shall be a blessing. 3I will bless those who bless you, and I will curse him who curses you; and in you all the families of the earth shall be blessed." Genesis 12.1-3

6. **To steal that which belongs to God.**

   "10Bring all the tithes into the storehouse, that there may be food in My house, and try Me now in this," says the LORD of hosts, "If I will not open for you the windows of heaven and pour out for you such blessing

that there will not be room enough to receive it. [11]"And I will rebuke the devourer for your sakes, so that he will not destroy the fruit of your ground, nor shall the vine fail to bear fruit for you in the field," says the LORD of hosts; [12]And all nations will call you blessed, for you will be a delightful land," says the LORD of hosts."
Malachi 3.10-12

For example, those who do not tithe or give offerings to God sometimes ask why things are not going well with their finances. It is because a curse has come upon them for not giving God what is rightfully his.

7. **Injustices:** Especially when the victim is weak, widowed, orphan, impoverished or a foreigner. God will judge those who harm these people.

8. **Hereditary curses:** Curses we carry in the bloodline such as incest, sickness, divorce, bad temper, rejection and sexual curses.

People often ask why they are always impoverished. Why are they sick? Why is their son or daughter a homosexual? Why are there so many divorces in their family? Why are their children using drugs?

In life, there is always a cause and effect. Instead of looking for solutions in the branches, we need to go to the root of the problem. As in the case of the spider and the spider web, there are many pastors who are trying to solve people's problems superficially, not realizing that they are treating the web and not the spider. They need to kill the spider, that is, to cast out the generational curses.

Steps to break curses and be free:

1. Recognize your sins and the sins of your ancestors, accepting responsibility for them. Repent, confess, and ask for forgiveness. The ancient prophets did this often; they stood in the place of the people and the nation, asking God for forgiveness.

2. Break every curse in the name of Jesus and by the blood of the Lamb. Call it by its name and cancel it with your mouth.

3. Order every spirit of the enemy behind the curse to leave your life and your family.

4. Declare out loud that you are free. Do it again and again until you are certain in your heart that God has set you free.

   "13Christ has redeemed us from the curse of the law, having become a curse for us (for it is written, "Cursed is everyone who hangs on a tree")." Galatians 3.13

When a person in willing to break a curse, obey God, and stand firm in every one of His promises, then the blessings will follow.

Areas that Need Deliverance

Sometimes, believers need deliverance in a specific area of their lives, such as mental health. In order to minister effectively, it is necessary to visit each area and break the power the enemy has in that specific area. There are eight areas in which deliverance and inner healing should be ministered. In this chapter we will study each one.

1. Mental and emotional problems

These are disturbances that persist in the mind and emotions. Some of the most common are: resentment, hatred, anger, fear, self-pity, depression, mental torment, worries, jealousy, inferiority and insecurity, confusion and doubt.

2. Sexual Problems

These oppressions are a result of sexual practices outside marriage. Common problems are unclean sexual thoughts and actions. These include: fornication, adultery, lust, masturbation, pornography, prostitution, abortion, incest, sexual fantasies, and sexual deviations such as homosexuality, lesbianism, bestiality, exhibitionism, sadism and masochism.

3. Problems with the Occult

Every method of seeking supernatural knowledge, wisdom, guidance and power outside of God is prohibited. Occult practices include witchcraft, spiritualism, predicting the future, palm or card reading, black or white magic, religious sects and practices such as Jehovah's Witnesses and Mormons, meditation, yoga, karate, Santeria, hypnotism, ouija boards, levitation, horoscopes and masonry.

4. Problems With Addictions

The most common addictions are nicotine, alcohol, gluttony, sex, compulsive exercise and drugs. There are people who are enslaved to drugs. Even though they want to stop using them, they are unable because something stronger than themselves is controlling them.

5. Physical Infirmities

The spirits of sickness cause many infirmities or illnesses. When a demon of sickness is cast out, there should also be prayer for complete healing. There is a close relationship between deliverance and inner healing. Some infirmities are healed instantly when the unclean spirit is cast out. These include epilepsy, arthritis, asthma, deafness and blindness.

"11And behold, there was a woman who had a spirit of infirmity eighteen years, and she was bent over and could in no way raise herself up." Luke 13.11

6. Problems With The Tongue

The uncontrolled use of the tongue includes lying, cursing, blasphemy, criticizing and gossip.

7. Problems With Forms of Control

These occur in people who have compromised their souls. For example, it is caused by contact with false religions such as Jehovah's Witnesses or Mormons, or pacts with the enemy. Manipulation is passed from one person to the other, such as parents to children, husbands to wives and vice versa.

8. Rejection – "The Syndrome of Triple Rejection"

When a person is rejected in his childhood, adolescence or adulthood, he requires ministering in the following three areas: the root of rejection, self-rejection and fear of rejection.

Clues to detect if someone is under demonic influences:

- **Who is in control?** Is the person completely in control or does she constantly say, "I have prayed, confessed, begged, fasted, and can't get victory over this sin." When these are not enough, there are demonic influences over the person. In other words, the person cannot control the problem alone.

- **A feeling of false hopelessness** is not merely the lack of hope; it encompasses resentment, hatred and bitterness, even if the person does not confess these feelings.

- **Divine revelation**. Every time we minister inner healing and deliverance, it is necessary to depend completely and absolutely on the Holy Spirit. Believers often forget incidents that require confession in order for them to be completely delivered. The Holy Spirit will lead the way and reveal the matter.

- **The value of specific questions**. It is very important, and absolutely necessary to ask specific questions that help identify each problem.

- **Body language**. Those who minister deliverance should be attentive to physical signs that could indicate a problem, perhaps one of which the person is unaware. He may be in denial or have forgotten to mention it. These signs include lack of eye contact, nervousness, the smell of alcohol or nicotine, uneasiness, and others.

- **Recognizable symptoms.** When Jesus was here on earth, people were quite familiar with demons. For instance, the woman from Phoenicia pleaded with Jesus to cast out an unclean spirit from her daughter. She said, "My daughter is seriously tormented by a demon." How did she know this? By the child's symptoms.

When a person has a problem in the flesh, it is possible to control the habit by living and walking in the Spirit. But if there is a demonic influence, even when the person fasts and prays, he will find it difficult to overcome the problem on his own.

"24From there He arose and went to the region of Tyre and Sidon. And He entered a house and wanted no one to know it, but He could not be hidden. 25For a woman whose young daughter had an unclean spirit heard about Him, and she came and fell at His feet. 26The woman was a Greek, a Syro-Phoenician by birth, and she kept asking Him to cast the demon out of her daughter. 27But Jesus said to her, "Let the children be filled first, for it is not good to take the children's bread and throw it to the little dogs." 28And she answered and said to Him, "Yes, Lord, yet even the little dogs under the table eat from the children's crumbs." 29Then He said to her, "For this saying go your way; the demon has gone out of your daughter." 30And when she had come to her house, she found the demon gone out, and her daughter lying on the bed." Mark 7.24-30

Who needs inner healing and deliverance?

- Those who were given up for adoption or whose parents contemplated abortion.

- Individuals who were abandoned or rejected by their parents.

- Orphans or those who have been rejected.

- People who were abused, raped or sexually molested as children.

- Individuals with chronic, lifelong illnesses or a history of sickness in their bloodline such as cancer or diabetes.

- People with uncontrollable habits who have fasted, prayed, and tried everything without success.

- Those with persistent and uncontrollable fears of all types.

- People who suffer rejection, depression, loneliness, desperation and suicidal tendencies.

- Those who are frigid, obsessed with sexual desires, or those who have impure thoughts about people of the same sex.

- Individuals suffering from guilt and condemnation, or those who have trouble forgiving others.

- Those who have difficulty forgiving others.

- People who have resentment or blasphemous thoughts against God. They will often ask, "God, why did you let this happen?"

- People who were in war zones or combat.

- Individuals who are constantly angry, shy, ashamed or chronic liars.

- People living as homosexuals, lesbians, or transsexuals.

- Those who practice, or have practiced, the occult, satanic worship, astrology or Santeria.

- Individuals who belonged to, or participate in, religious sects.

- Those who took part in, or had an abortion.

- Individuals with a compulsive desire to destroy others; those who gossip, curse or complain.

- Those with hatred or bitterness toward another person, race or ethnic group.

- Those who are easily depressed.

- Those diagnosed with schizophrenia.

- People who are exposed to pornography, or addicted to alcohol, drugs or food, or are sexually perverted.

- Intensely jealous people.

- People who practice yoga or martial arts.

- Individuals with masturbation problems, lust of the eyes and mind, or a history of sexual perversion.

- People who are been rebellious or disobedient.

- People who killed someone, or have the desire to do so.

- Individuals who hate children.

These are only some of the people who need the ministry of inner healing and deliverance; there may very well be others who are not mentioned here. We strongly emphasize the importance of asking the one being ministered specific questions, because they will guide those who are ministering, to the areas that require special attention.

When we to for deliverance, it is very important to be honest and transparent with the person leading the deliverance for it to be effective, it is also important to recognize and confess any of the areas mentioned above, it is the only way the power of God can set us free.

CHAPTER

﹏﹏﹏ 14 ﹏﹏﹏

Schizophrenia

Schizophrenia is a very common problem. Mental health authorities believe there are about 50 million schizophrenics in the United States. This is one in every eight people. Schizophrenics constitute about half of the population in psychiatric hospitals in the United States.

What is schizophrenia?

Schizophrenia is a disturbance, distortion or deterioration in the development of the personality. It is a dual personality that causes instability.

"⁸He is a double-minded man, unstable in all his ways."
James 1.8

"For being as he is a man of two minds, hesitating, doubtful, unstable. He is unreliable *and* uncertain about everything he thinks, feels, and decides."

Unfortunately, many ministers refer church members suffering from this problem to psychiatrists or psychologists, because they have yet to discover the solution for schizophrenia. Often, they use the world's methods in the church, overlooking the fact that Jesus gave believers the power and authority to free the people from any type of bondage.

The schizophrenic's personality cannot develop properly due to demonic interference. Demonic spirits of **rejection** are operating **internally,** while **rebellious** personalities manifest themselves **externally** through the person's behavior. These spirits take control, causing the personality to split –internally, as well as, externally.

It is a terrible emotional shock for someone to discover that much of his personality is not his real "I", and he may become fearful of discovering his true personality. He needs time to adjust and understand the truth about false demonic personalities. Schizophrenia begins with **rejection**, which in turn opens the door to **rebellion**. This pattern begins in childhood and is sometimes inherited.

The three principal areas that a schizophrenic needs to overcome to be set free are **rejection, rebellion and the root of bitterness**. To the extent that these areas are conquered, the "house", that is, the life of the affected person, becomes capable of giving and receiving love, submitting to true authority, and forgiving those who hurt them, regardless of the circumstances. When these three areas are conquered, related spirits lose their power.

Deliverance of schizophrenics requires strong commitment and compassion; it is the most demanding and difficult type of deliverance. It is often a progressive deliverance, requiring cooperation on the part of the affected person.

The spirits operating in a person with rejection include fantasies, lust, suicide, guilt, pride, loneliness, fear, abandonment, self-pity, inordinate affection for animals and self-rejection. The spirits operating in a rebellious person include selfishness, pride, violence, stubbornness, bitterness, anger and resentment.

The schizophrenic is hesitant, insecure, indecisive and unstable. Their instability makes it difficult for them to confront or resolve problems without going deeper into their rejection and rebelliousness. A double-minded person, or dual personality, is unstable in all his ways.

What is the solution for schizophrenia? The solution is deliverance in the name of Jesus and the anointing of the Holy Spirit. This is the only way the person can attain a stable personality in Jesus Christ.

Deliverance for Children

The truth of the Word of God teaches that children can be influenced by demons, as in the case of the epileptic boy and the daughter of the Syro-Phoenician woman.

Let us keep in mind that children are not able to seek help on their own, so it is the responsibility of the parents as the head of household, to seek deliverance on their behalf.

Can children be influenced by demons? Yes.

"37Now it happened on the next day, when they had come down from the mountain, that a great multitude met Him. 38Suddenly a man from the multitude cried out, saying, 'Teacher, I implore you, look on my son, for he is my only child. 39And behold, a spirit seizes him, and he suddenly cries out; it convulses him so that he foams at the mouth; and it departs from him with great difficulty, bruising him. 40So I implored your disciples to cast it out, but they could not."41Then Jesus answered and said, "O faithless and perverse generation, how long shall I be with you and bear with you? Bring your son here.' 42And as he was still coming, the demon threw him down and convulsed him. Then Jesus rebuked the unclean spirit, healed the child, and gave him back to his father." Luke 9.37-42

"²⁴From there He arose and went to the region of Tyre and Sidon. And He entered a house and wanted no one to know it, but He could not be hidden. ²⁵For a woman whose young daughter had an unclean spirit heard about Him, and she came and fell at His feet. ²⁶The woman was a Greek, a Syro-Phoenician by birth, and she kept asking Him to cast the demon out of her daughter. ²⁷But Jesus said to her, "Let the children be filled first, for it is not good to take the children's bread and throw it to the little dogs." ²⁸And she answered and said to Him, "Yes, Lord, yet even the little dogs under the table eat from the children's crumbs." ²⁹Then He said to her, "For this saying go your way; the demon has gone out of your daughter." ³⁰And when she had come to her house, she found the demon gone out, and her daughter lying on the bed." Mark 7.24-30

Deliverance is not a substitute for:

➢ The love a child needs.
➢ A stable home.
➢ Education, discipline, and appropriate upbringing.
➢ Protection, care, affection, tenderness, acceptance and security.

Parents can and should minister deliverance to their children because they are their spiritual covering and the authority over them.

How to minister to children according to their age.

▪ Since birth until four years of age, it is not necessary to give any explanation regarding ministering, since demons are not involved in the child's will.

- From four to six years of age, one provides a short and simple explanation to the child.

- From six to twelve years old, their will is involved and their cooperation required. One ministers the same way one does to an adult, except that one uses a simple vocabulary so that the child understands.

One should be calm and minister with tranquility when addressing a child. One has to distinguish between the child and the demon, treating the demon firmly, but being compassionate with the child. When ministering, do not become distracted because the child cries or tries to seek comfort, keep him calm. Do not shout, as you can frighten him.

Forms of satanic oppression:

- **Bondage**. The enemy stops them from doing what is right, such as apologizing when they know they have done something wrong, forgiving others, being honest, obedient, respectful or diligent.

- **Domination**. The enemy makes them do things they know are wrong and do not want to do. For example: Getting angry, being stubborn, deceitful, cheating, etc.

- **Oppression**. Satan often harasses children with different kinds of fears. He can make them anxious for no apparent reason and is opposed to the development of their spiritual life.

- **Afflictions.** A spirit may cause children to have accidents, difficulties, frequent illnesses and allergies of all kinds.

- **Parents can bring oppression to their children**. Many parents overlook the fact that they can be the basic cause of their children's problems. Parents must free themselves of their own problems before they can minister deliverance to their children. Deliverance of children can begin when the parents themselves start seeking deliverance from demonic oppression through Jesus Christ.

These are some parents' demonic oppressions that may affect their children:

- **Generational curses.** This includes occult practices, witchcraft, various addictions, anxiety, preoccupation, depression, mental problems, suicide, illicit sexual practices, religious spirits, sickness, allergies and rejection.

- **Oppression prior to salvation**. In addition to generational curses, children can be oppressed because of their parents' sins before they were saved. If parents are not delivered after experiencing salvation, demonic activity can influence their children.

- **Family possessions that have satanic origin**. Sometimes parents keep religious objects, pornographic videos or magazines, violent or horror movies, or toys such as Power Rangers, Pokémon, The Smurfs, Ninja Turtles and others. These must be removed from the home as soon as possible.

How to Minister Deliverance to Children

Never use the word demon when speaking to children about their problems; instead use terms such as "spiritual influences", or "bad things that happen to families." Avoid causing fear. If you intend to pray for deliverance, take your time and discuss what is about to happen with the child.

Steps to take in praying for children:

➢ **Who should pray for children?** Parents who have already been delivered should pray and deliver their own children. Parents have more authority to pray for their children than anyone else because they are their spiritual covering.

➢ **How to pray.** Lay hands on the forehead of the child, or on their head. If the child is older than five, guide him in renouncing his sin and to pray. If the child does not want to cooperate or renounce, the adult should renounce for them. Deliverance will take place.

➤ **Why pray.** Write a list of the obvious problems the child has, such as: hereditary problems, addictions, mental problems, and rejection. You should pray as follows: "spirit of anger, I order you to let go of my child in the name of Jesus!" "Spirit of rejection I command you to leave my child in the name of Jesus!" Name each one, one after the other.

➤ **What to do during prayer.** Speak to the Lord simply and naturally, thanking him for his complete work on the cross, and because he came to destroy the works of the devil. Then, in the name of Jesus, bind and cast out every spirit on your list.

Remember, it is easier to cast out demons from children than from adults because demons are not as deeply rooted in children.

➤ **How to end a deliverance session**

  ▪ **Cleansing.** With your hands still on the child's head, ask the Lord to cleanse each part of your child's personality where a demon has persisted. This includes his mind, heart, will, and different parts of his body, especially the sexual organs, respiratory system and in some cases, the chest.

- **Fullness.** Ask the Lord to fill your child with His love, His presence and His peace.

- **Healing.** Appropriate physical healing, especially in parts of the body that may have been affected.

Consistent prayer is essential for our children. Remember that they are more receptive and tend to absorb spiritual influences easier than adults. Clear understanding of these principles will help you comprehend that children need to continually receive the orientation of God's Word and the touch of His presence.

How to Minister Deliverance

I n this chapter you will learn how to minister deliverance. At this point, you will need to apply everything you have learned in this book. There are different methods in use today, but in every case it is very important to depend on the guidance of the Holy Spirit of God.

Before studying the steps to minister deliverance, let us examine some of the obstacles that prevent many people from receiving it.

Obstacles to Receiving Deliverance

The majority of the people who received deliverance through our ministry were freed successfully, with a few exceptions. Why exceptions? Because obstacles prevented them from being set free. We will examine some of these:

1. **Lack of repentance:** When there is no recognition nor genuine pain for having had offended God, it is difficult to feel the desire to change, therefore, God cannot work. But if there is genuine repentance, the Holy Spirit can work and there will be a change of direction, not only in the mind, but also in the heart. If there is genuine repentance, that person will turn his life around 180 degrees. Jesus

said: *"Repent and believe" (Mark 1.15).* No one can believe without first repenting.

2. **Lack of desperation or desire:** The person should be fed up with his condition to the point of hating it. The fear of God should fill his heart. He must hate evil, and take a stand against sin or failure. Until people come to hate whatever binds them, God cannot set them free. Pornography is an example. I have prayed for people to be set free from this bondage once, but after they were delivered, I had to pray for them again. Deliverance is for people who desperately want to be free.

3. **Selfishness and the desire for attention:** Some people feel ignored and unimportant. They are really looking for attention from other people. Deep in their hearts, they do not truly want to be free. If they were to be delivered, they would not give the glory to God.

4. **Not confessing a specific sin:** A sin that is not confessed leaves the door open for the enemy, and as long as he has a place to stay, he will not depart.

"9That was the true Light which gives light to every man coming into the world." John 1.9

"27nor give place to the devil." Ephesians 4.27

5. **Part of a bigger battle:** The enemy does not want to let certain people go because they are strategic people, called to be future channels of blessing for many. Once they are delivered, they will become instruments of salvation for their families or many others, because of their testimony and God's great purpose in their lives.

6. **Lack of forgiveness:** If a person does not forgive, it is impossible for God to deliver him. Forgiveness is essential for deliverance to take place. If it does not happen, nothing else will work either.

7. **Disbelief and doubt:** Some people ask to be delivered, but they do not actually believe. It is important to remember that deliverance is received by faith.

8. **Unholy relationships and ties:** Some people who seek deliverance are still attached to illicit relationships, and that prevents them from being delivered. For example, this is true of people who are practicing adultery or fornication. They should not attempt to receive deliverance until they renounce their sin and completely leave the sin behind.

Some obstacles that ministers Encounter while ministering deliverance:

- **Unclean vessels:** Ministers that try to deliver someone else from bondage will fail, if they suffer from a similar bondage.

- **Lack of prayer life:** *Matthew 17.21* say: *"This kind does not go out except with prayer and fasting."* Additional power is necessary to cast out certain demons. This can only be accomplished through profound prayer and fasting. Unfortunately, deliverance cannot be ministered if there is no time for prayer, the Word of God, and total dependence on the Holy Spirit.

- **Lack of compassion:** Before ministering deliverance, completely identify with the pain of the other person, support her, and make it easy for her to receive her deliverance.

- **Incorrect techniques:** Some ministers get involved in manipulation and control of people and do not rely on the Lord.

- **Forgetting that the cause may not be spiritual.** some problems may have organic causes. These include poor nutrition, hormonal or brain disorders, or a work of the flesh rather than a satanic oppression.

Things that should not be done during deliverance:

- Do not pat the person on the back, or say: "I know exactly how you feel, surrender it to the Lord." If they knew how to surrender to the Lord, they would not need your help.

- Do not try to cast out all demons in one session. I recommend that each session last no more than two hours, otherwise both the minister and the person being counseled will become exhausted.

- Do not become a permanent crutch. We should teach people to deliver themselves, or to depend upon God and not on the minister.

- Be cautious about physical contact.

- Do not minister deliverance when you are tired.

How to prepare to be a minister of deliverance:

Every person who intends to minister deliverance, should keep the following in mind:

- **Submit yourself to deliverance first:** Remember, we need to be delivered first, before we are able to deliver others, we should submit to a deliverance ourselves, not just once, but as often as necessary.

- **Be baptized with the Holy Spirit:** This will help you to be open to the manifestations of the Holy Spirit.

- **Use the weapons God has given you:** Put on the spiritual armor.

"11Put on the whole armor of God, that you may be able to stand against the wiles of the devil." Ephesians 6.11

Know the power there is in the name of Jesus, seek and have the anointing of God and His authority. Be familiar with the Word of God, which is powerful and a double-edged sword.

"12For the word of God is living and powerful, and sharper than any two-edged sword, piercing even to the division of soul and spirit, and of joints and marrow, and is a discerner of the thoughts and intents of the heart." Hebrews 4.12

Steps to Minister Deliverance

1. **Make sure the person is born again:** If the person is not born again, present the plan of salvation and invite him to receive Christ, otherwise, his condition will get worse if you try to minister deliverance.

2. **Prepare the person:** Explain important points, such as:

   - They must desire to be set free.

   - They must be willing to forgive those who have hurt them and caused them problems and pain. If this is not possible, postpone deliverance until they are ready to forgive.

- They need to be ready to renounce sin, break bad habits, separate from others who are living in iniquity, and do anything necessary to be delivered and healed.

- They should promise to maintain a close relationship with God, go to church, read the Bible and pray.

3. **Compose a questionnaire:** You may use the questions in this book or compose your own comprehensive questionnaire to assist you in ministering effectively. Ask the person being delivered to answer questions in five or more areas of their lives. This will help you discover the roots of many problems such as rejection, emotional and mental conditions, spiritual influences (e.g., witchcraft or the occult), sexual practices, lust, addictions, generational curses, etc. Christian leaders may also contact our ministry for a copy of our questionnaire.

The questionnaire may not cover every area, so it is important to write down what the person being delivered tells you. Make a list of the names of the spirits that are influencing the person. For example, if a person was sexually abused, the spirits that could be influencing him or her are lust, adultery, fornication, sodomy and frigidity or impotence.

4. **Repentance and forgiveness:** Once you have ga-thered all the information, lead the person to renounce, repent and ask the Lord for forgiveness for the sins committed. For instance, if she has been hurt, she needs to ask God for forgiveness for any judgment and resentment she has held in her heart, and also to forgive those who hurt her.

5. **Renouncing:** This is the stage in which we lead someone to renounce each problem and spirit on the list. Why should the person seeking de-liverance renounce them? Because when they renounce these things, they are closing doors and canceling all legal rights the enemy has over them.

    In other words, when a person sins, legal rights are given to the enemy to influence their lives. That right must be cancelled and the only means to do it is by renouncing it. The person being delivered needs to repeat what the minister asks him or her to say. Say something like this: "I renounce every spirit of rejection operating in my life and cast it out in the name of Jesus Christ." Then the believer repeats it after you.

    "12Teaching us that, denying ungodliness and worldly lusts, we should live soberly, righteously, and godly..."
    Titus 2.12

6. **A prayer of spiritual warfare:** Once the person verbally renounces all bondages, repeating every-

thing the minister has guided him or her to say, the minister conducts the prayer of spiritual warfare, casting out every spirit, generational curse or emotional problem. Pray for the person firmly and with authority.

For example, "Heavenly Father, I cast out every spirit of rejection, every spirit of fear in the name of Jesus. By the blood of the Lamb I bind you and cast you out of the life of (the name of the person). Right now I order you to let go of this person."

How do you know when spirits leave a person? They yawn, vomit, cough, sigh, roar, exhale, scream, burp, cry, or become short of breath. These are only some of the signs. This does not mean that if none of these signs occur, that the person was not delivered. Many people are delivered with no physical manifestations whatsoever. If the individual becomes violent, order the demons to be quiet and not to move, in the name of Jesus. Never allow the spirits to control a deliverance session.

7. **Pray for cleansing:** Ask the Lord to cleanse every area of the individual's personality that the spirits may have harmed. This includes the mind, heart and will, as well as any affected part of the body, especially the sexual organs.

You may pray something like this: "Heavenly Father, I ask you to please cleanse all areas of the mind of this person that were harmed by the enemy. Lord, cleanse the sexual organs by the blood of Jesus, as well as his soul, and his will, in the name of Jesus. Amen."

8. **Pray for the fullness of the Spirit:** Remember, when the spirits leave a person, there will be a void left behind. That empty place needs to be filled by God. Ask the Lord to fill them with his presence, peace and love.

Your prayer may be along these lines: "Heavenly Father, I ask that you fill (name of person) with your peace, love and presence. Lord, I ask that every void that the spirits have left be filled with the Holy Spirit, in the name of Jesus. Amen."

Sometimes it is important for the individual to appropriate physical healing, especially in those parts of the body that were affected. We have ministered to people with vision problems, who, once the spirit was cast out, were completely healed. Some people need more than one deliverance session, which should not last more than two hours. On the other hand, we have also seen cases of people who were totally delivered in one session.

Self-deliverance

People often ask if they are able to do self-deliverance. We certainly can deliver ourselves by following the steps described above, except for the fact that no one is there to guide us.

God has given believers the power and authority to cast out demons from other people's lives as well as from their own. How do we do it? By following the steps listed above.

How to Maintain Our Deliverance

1. Develop a consistent prayer life.

Jesus said to keep watch and remain in prayer, thus preventing us from falling into temptation. One attribute that prayer develops is self-control. This virtue will help us to resist temptations and to stand firm.

"41Watch and pray, lest you enter into temptation. The spirit indeed is willing, but the flesh is weak."
Matthew 26.41

"17...pray without ceasing." 1 Thessalonians 5.17

2. Read and study the Word of God.

It is very important to remain in the Scriptures, because the Word fills the void left after deliverance. The Word of God is the anchor of the soul, and no one can remain free of temptation and sin, if time and dedication are not given to reading the Word, studying it, and meditating on it. Begin to confess biblical verses about being delivered over your life.

"¹²For the word of God is living and powerful, and sharper than any two-edged sword, piercing even to the division of soul and spirit, and of joints and marrow, and is a discerner of the thoughts and intents of the heart. Hebrews 4.12

"¹⁰⁵Your word is a lamp to my feet and a light to my path." Psalm 119.105

3. Congregate in the church.

Sheep who separate from the flock are the most vulnerable to the enemy's destruction. Congregating will allow you to share and develop friendships among brothers and sisters who can help you grow spiritually. You need to submit to the authority of the pastor, and to give an account of how you are doing after receiving ministry.

4. Crucify the flesh and the ego.

Take your cross and follow the Lord Jesus Christ. Break every old pattern and habit that kept you attached to unclean spirits. Be prepared to deny yourself and to crucify the flesh. If the desires and appetites of the flesh are not surrendered at the cross, a door will remain open for the demons to return.

"²³Then He said to them all, "If anyone desires to come after Me, let him deny himself, and take up his cross daily, and follow Me." Luke 9.23

"³⁸And he who does not take his cross and follow after Me is not worthy of Me." Matthew 10.38

5. Separate yourself from sin.

To separate from sin implies separation from places, people and circumstances that induce us to sin. This includes getting rid of magazines and all other objects related to former practices.

"¹⁵My son, do not walk in the way with them, keep your foot from their path." Proverbs 1.15

"¹³He who covers his sins will not prosper, but whoever confesses and forsakes them will have mercy." Proverbs 28.13

6. Put on the armor of God.

Put on the armor with prayer and the confession of our mouth. It is important to put it on before leaving home, one piece at a time. Remember, God will not put it on for you; you have to do this yourself.

"¹⁰Finally, my brethren, be strong in the Lord and in the power of His might." Ephesians 6.10

7. Plead the blood of Jesus.

During prayer, always plead the blood of Jesus. Use it to protect your mind, soul and family. The blood of Jesus creates a circle of protection that the enemy cannot penetrate. It is necessary to plead the blood and to put on the spiritual armor, daily.

"[11]And they overcame him by the blood of the Lamb and by the word of their testimony, and they did not love their lives to the death." Revelation 12.11

8. Develop a forgiving spirit.

One of the biggest inroads the enemy uses to oppress believers is resentment and lack of forgiveness in their hearts. This attracts demons; so after forgiving someone, understand that you live in a world where this is bound to happen over and over again. Immediately after being hurt, forgive. Develop a forgiving spirit (*Matthew 18.21-35*).

9. Resist the devil.

God has given all of us spiritual weapons, so use them and resist the devil. These weapons are the blood, the Word, fasting, worship and prayer.

"[7]Therefore, submit to God. Resist the devil and he will flee from you." James 4.7

10. Renew the mind.

Demons will try to return to a person who has an undisciplined lifestyle. The mind is a battlefield. You need to renounce bad thoughts and bring every thought captive to the obedience of Christ. Remember, you have been given power and authority by God to cast out demons from your mind and to rebuke any attack that comes into your life.

"⁴For the weapons of our warfare are not carnal but mighty in God for pulling down strongholds."
2 Corinthians 10.4

How important it is to know that the Word of God promises to free everyone who is enslaved and oppressed by demonic forces. The name of Jesus is the ultimate authority that can break the bondage of darkness and to completely deliver all who believe in Him.

CHAPTER

❧❧❧ *17* ❧❧❧

Spiritual Housecleaning

D eliverance practices are often taken to extremes, but that is not the purpose of this chapter. Throughout the years, we have seen believers be under persistent attack without understanding why. Often it is because they have given legal rights to the enemy by keeping objects and things that originate in the occult.

"¹⁷This became known both to all Jews and Greeks dwelling in Ephesus; and fear fell on them all, and the name of the Lord Jesus was magnified. ¹⁸And many who had believed came confessing and telling their deeds." Acts 19.17, 18

"¹²Therefore the children of Israel could not stand before their enemies, but turned their backs before their enemies, because they have become doomed to destruction. Neither will I be with you anymore, unless you destroy the accursed from among you. ¹³Up, sanctify the people, and say, Sanctify yourselves against to morrow: for thus saith the LORD God of Israel, There is an accursed thing in the midst of thee, O Israel: thou canst not stand before thine enemies, until ye take away the accursed thing from among you." Joshua 7.12, 13

Symptoms of a house that is spiritually contaminated:

Symptoms include frequent illness, nightmares, constant fighting and divisions, lack of peace, demonic appearances, movement of objects with no explanation, bad odors, habitual nausea and headaches.

"⁸For you were once darkness, but now you are light in the Lord. Walk as children of light ⁹(for the fruit of the Spirit is in all goodness, righteousness, and truth), ¹⁰finding out what is acceptable to the Lord. ¹¹And have no fellowship with the unfruitful works of darkness, but rather expose them." Ephesians 5.8-11

Articles that need to be removed and burnt:

➤ Materials used in witchcraft or occult activities

➤ Antiques with unknown backgrounds

➤ Materials such as ouija boards, dragon games, Buddha figures, yoga books and Hindu objects

➤ Artifacts of Oriental worship, New Age books

➤ Quartz stones, candles, items used for good luck

➤ The rosary, figures of saints

➤ Astrology books, Tarot cards, crystal balls and pendulums

➤ CDs, cassettes and posters of rock music

➤ Arts, crafts and pictures with demonic representations.

- Material related to sects such as the Mormons, Jehovah's Witnesses, Freemasonry and the Rosicrucian

- Souvenirs from other countries that contain images of idols

- Good luck charms, fetishes or religious objects

- Demonic, violent, pornographic movies or videos

- Images or statutes of angels, or elephants used for good luck

- Images that represent the goddess Diana, queen of heaven.

Sometimes we wonder why certain things happen in our homes. Often, the reason is because objects of demonic origin are being kept there.

It is very important to clean our homes. Go through your house, looking through all the closets and rooms, asking the Holy Spirit to show you what things are not pleasing to God. Then throw them away. Be confident that He will show you.

Conclusion

We have reviewed the fundamental issues of deliverance; and I trust that this will continue to motivate you to seek God more and the freedom that He wants for your life. Will to achieve it, not only for yourself, but also your family. When you are free, you will feel happy and will be a person of testimony and of hope for many others that today feel empty, confused, sic, tormented and without hope of change.

Deliverance is the path to achieving happiness in Christ. He already gave His life for us, now we have to remove the bandages and bondages from the past and follow Him in freedom. Jesus is the way, the truth and the life; follow Him, depend on Him, and allow Him to reign in every aspect of your life. Amen!

Sinner's Prayer

Right now, wherever you are, you can receive the gift of eternal life, through Jesus Christ. Please, accom-pany me in this prayer, and repeat out loud.

"Father, I recognize that I am a sinner, and that my sin separates me from you. I repent from all my sins, and I voluntarily, confess Jesus as my Lord and Savior; and I believe that He died for my sins. I believe, with all of my heart, that God, the Father, resurrected from the dead. Jesus, I ask that you come into my heart and change my life. I renounce any pact with the enemy; and if I were to die right now, I know that when I open my eyes, I will be in your arms. Amen!"

If this prayer expresses the sincere desire of your heart, observe what Jesus says regarding the decision that you have just made:

"9that if you confess with your mouth the Lord Jesus and believe in your heart that God has raised Him from the dead, you will be saved. 10For with the heart one believes unto righteousness, and with the mouth confession is made unto salvation." Romans 10.9, 10

"47Most assuredly, I say to you, he who believes in Me has everlasting life." John 6.47

Testimonies

First Testimony

The day of my deliverance was awesome. As usual, they started with the questionnaire. Time seemed to slip by and the ministers told me they would continue the next day.

As they continued with my deliverance they ordered the spirits to come out of me. I had a lot of spiritual strongholds, so my deliverance took longer than others. For instance, my family practiced witchcraft, since I am from the Dominican Republic and also have ancestors from Haiti. - Both countries practice voodoo and witchcraft. I also practiced *Santeria* with some Cuban friends who were *santeros* and others that were *babalaos.*

The day before we finished my deliverance, on my way to a meeting, and while on the expressway, I heard a voice say to me "I am going to kill you". Trucks were passing, I became disoriented and I lost my way. I was very scared, I prayed to the Lord, I covered myself with the blood of Jesus, and He took me home safely.

Finally the moment came to renounce everything that was holding me captive. When they dealt with the sexual areas, these were the ones that stunk the most. I started burping with a terrible smell. I was bound to masturbation since I was a child, and although I knew the Lord, I still practiced it. That day I was delivered, thanks to the Lord! My life has been transformed. Now I can pray and read the Word of God. At long last, I am in love with my Lord.

Second Testimony

I AM TOTALLY FREE! *"Therefore, he that the Lord sets free is free indeed". John 8.36*

This well known verse covers a marvelous and unimaginable truth through which I have been able to fully live, by Jesus' great love and mercy. I give Him all the praise and worship forever, Amen.

I can truly say that inner healing and deliverance are two powerful tools, in addition to prayer and the Word. I experimented what it felt like to be trapped in a deep abyss with no way out. It was not until much later that I was finally able to see a light which was the way to my total deliverance, as it says in *Psalm 103.1-5.*

I got to the church and requested what I now call my "divine appointment". The process began with the Lord, who used two precious servants, Ana and Maribel. They gave all of themselves, until with the help of the Holy Spirit, I was finally set free. My deliverance took several sessions, some lasted well

into the night, but as always, God provided everything we needed; I give Him all the glory!

I was emotionally destroyed. At the time, I was going
through the most difficult time that any man, or
woman, may have to experience. As the saying goes:
"dead in life". I was abandoned an abused, physically, as well as, emotionally. I had severe trauma
from my childhood fro which I was unable to recover
on my own. I considered suicide several times because in my mind, I thought I deserved it, after all, is
there anything else a troublemaker like me, deserves?

I was never able to finish what I started. I was rejected
in every way imaginable. My self-esteem was extremely low. I hated myself and felt guilty all the time. I
condemned myself, and thought that I was less than
other women. I felt I was a "good-for-nothing". I also
suffered various serious accidents. To make matters
worse, I was separated from the people I love the
most, my children, my family, and my country. I was
in unknown lands, far from God, and I did not have
many friends. I was also abandoned by my husband
who calls himself a Christian, and with whom I
served full time in ministry, back in our country; this
hurt me so much, that all I wanted to do was die.

Each session was like a movie. It was hard remem-
bering the situations I experienced in my childhood,
my teenage years, my adult life, and my marriage.
However, each time I had an appointment, it felt that

the load was getting lighter. That is what Lord says in *Mathew 11.30: "Because my yoke is easy and my burden is light."* These "divine appointments" I previously mentioned, changed my life completely.

I did a 180 degrees turn in my life, my face and the way I look, changed. All the strongholds, all the generational curses, and the painful traumas disappeared. This did not happen magically, but it did happen when I decided I was tired of the way I was living. Now I understand the importance or our attitude when we make decisions that are going to change the course of our lives.

I know the Lord forgives our mistakes, and in His eyes, we are greatly esteemed. Men may lie and abandon us, but in the Lord, we find the true and perfect love, (agape) the arm of a friend, of the husband, and the one person who is true.

After going through what I went through in my life, the traumas, the abandonment, rejection, separation, and divorce, I now know for certain that the only one who does not look at us as if we were a "third class citizen" is the Lord. He delivered me from all curses, I was healed, and today I am able to serve Him with all my heart. I am eternally grateful to Him, every single day, for loving me as I am.

Today, I give all of my love into what I consider to be the best ministry within the church, Evangelism. I have marvelous promises from God, and I know He will never abandon me. And when the enemy reminds me of situations that were settled at my deliverance, I am reminded of the fact that He healed me completely, and the reason I can say this is because when the memory of those past events no longer hurt me.

He calls us and He fulfills His purpose in us. I am now able to finish every project I start, and very soon, my children will be with me.

I encourage every woman man and child, not to allow the things in your life to take control of you. Take control of your surroundings. Take a new turn in your life through inner healing and deliverance, and use the authority given to you in the name of Jesus. Make forgiveness a lifestyle choice and you will see how wonderfully God will work in your heart. You will feel free, and you will find the peace that no one else can offer. I recommend that you go through the process of inner healing and deliverance; your life will never be the same again.

*Isaiah 43.19 "Behold, I am doing a new thing; now it springs forth; do you not perceive **and** know it **and** will you not give heed to it? I will even make ways in the wilderness and in the dessert."*

Third Testimony

One of the things that impacts me the most during the time that I have been ministering inner healing and deliverance, is to see the multiple generational curses that our brothers carry from their ancestors. A curse is like a dark shadow that follows a person. That is the way the enemy tries to steal all of our blessings. In *Deuteronomy 28.15* it says, *"And all these curses shall overcome you, and overtake you, until you perish."* *1 John 3.8, "⁸He who sins is of the devil, for the devil has sinned from the beginning. For this purpose the Son of God was manifested, that He might destroy the works of the devil."*

In *Mark 16.17* it says: *"and these signs will follow those who believe, in my name they shall cast out demons"* The first part of this verse clearly demonstrates that deliverance and inner healing is a ministry. One of the things that the Holy Spirit is guiding me to is to understand that deliverance is still as effective as when Jesus walked the earth.

I thank God for calling me to this ministry; it is a great privilege to serve Him. I also thank the Lord for trusting me with His beloved people, whom I am able to minister personally. Through the help of the Holy Spirit, I see them freely rejoice, delivered and filled with His peace.

May all the grace, the honor, and glory, be to our Heavenly Father. Amen!

Fourth Testimony

I reserve the right not to disclose the names of the people and of the countries where I have ministered inner healing and deliverance. We can write many testimonies of the changes in people's lives, and what held them in bondage, and the Glory will always belong to Him; the Lord has delivered them from their captors.

We may have a lot of knowledge, and attend all the seminars on deliverance, but we will always need to experience the practical and personal ministry of inner healing and deliverance.

God has granted me the privilege to minister deliverance to His people. I have had cases of people, who were still in bondage in certain sexual areas, even after they became believers. They tried to change on their own, but lacked the knowledge, and the proper ministry. Perhaps they also lacked the willingness to renounce to these influences. They were victims of their family's generational curses and of the consequence of sin. We have seen these people delivered and their lifestyles transformed.

Fifth Testimony

I remember the case of a man, a born again believer, with a series of problems in the financial, emotional, physical, and spiritual areas. When he was in the world, he had a ritual of spiritual occultism done in order to obtain economic power to make money. He drank the blood of a drug trafficker who had a lot of money and power in his country. We led him to renounce to all of this, and the pact was broken. We cast out each demon behind this pact, and saw him truly liberated and changed.

I also remember the case of a man, who at the age of 18 dedicated his head to Satan. It was a Santeria type of initiation, which his family had practiced for various generations. Consequently, he had serious drug problems. He was also a violent person. Demons spoke to him and offered him power. - We ministered his deliverance because he wanted to be free. It was very strong. During the actual deliverance the enemy brought great oppression to his head, since he had dedicated it to Satan several years before. God has completely delivered him and he is a different man, completely free.

Also, in another country, I ministered deliverance to a man who was a believer. He had various generational curses from several previous generations. He was sexually abused, raped and practiced pedophilia. His grandfather abused him, and his brothers. Later, a cousin also abused him. Consequently, this boy abused other boys as he grew up. The spirit of homo-sexuality totally possessed him during his adoles-cence. Years later, he accepted Jesus as his Lord and Savior, but he was never ministered inner healing and deliverance, he was taught that when he came to the Lord, all things passed away and were made new. However, he was still tormented by spiritual in-fluences and thoughts of the past. He was unable to pray or worship the Lord. After we ministered deliverance, all the demonic influences fled. This brother was filled with the Spirit and able to cry in the presence of God; he was delivered.

Churches of the Lord Jesus Christ that properly minister inner healing and deliverance will have healthy congregations in all areas, including the physical, emotional, spiritual and financial areas. They will be better able to fulfill the purpose of God, as they serve the Lord and help others.

Bibliography

Baker Encyclopedia of Psychologyogist. (Fuente bibliográfica utilizada para "Los Mecanismos de Defensa").

Biblia Plenitud. 1960 Reina-Valera Revision, ISBN: 089922279X, Editorial Caribe, Miami, Florida.

Diccionario Español a Inglés, Inglés a Español. Editorial Larousse S.A., impreso en Dinamarca, Núm. 81, México, ISBN: 2-03-420200-7, ISBN: 70-607-371-X, 1993.

Eckhardt, John. Liberación y Guerra Espiritual. Pages 33-34, 39, 50, 75.

Eckhardt, John. Déjanos Solos, los Gritos de los Demonios. Pages 13-16.

Eckhardt, John. Identificando y Rompiendo Maldiciones. Page 1.

Expanded Edition the Amplified Bible. Zondervan Bible Publishers. ISBN: 0-31095168-2, 1987 – lockman foundation USA.

Gibson, Noel & Phyl. Evicting Demonic Intruders. ISBN: 1-87436709-4. Pages 100-101, 133, 136-137.

Hammond, Frank. Cerdos en la Sala. Publisher: Impact Christian Books Publication, ISBN: 0892280271, Pages 45,48-49, 50-53, 144-145, 154.

Marzullo, Frank. *Deliverance & Spiritual Warfare Manual*. Crusaders Ministries Publisher. ISBN: 0963056778

Prince, Derek. *They Shall Expel Demons*. Chosen Books Publisher. ISBN: 0800792602. Pages 18-22, 98- 101, 165-166, 230.

Prince, Derek. *Blessing or Curses*. Chosen Books Publisher. ISBN: 0800792807, pages 45-47, 52-53, 56, 58.

Reina-Valera 1995 - Edición de Estudio, (Estados Unidos de América: Sociedades Bíblicas Unidas) 1998.

Strong James, LL.D, S.T.D., *Concordancia Strong Exhaustiva de la Biblia*, Editorial Caribe, Inc., Thomas Nelson, Inc., Publishers, Nashville, TN - Miami, FL, EE.UU., 2002. ISBN: 0-89922-382-6.

The New American Standard Version. Zordervan Publishing Company, ISBN: 0310903335, pages 255-266.

The Tormont Webster's Illustrated Encyclopedic Dictionary. ©1990 Tormont Publications. Pages 255-266.

Vine, W.E. *Diccionario Expositivo de las Palabras del Antiguo Testamento y Nuevo Testamento*. Editorial Caribe, Inc./División Thomas Nelson, Inc., Nashville, TN, ISBN: 0-89922-495-4, 1999.

Bibliography

Wagner Doris M. and Doris G. *How to Cast out Demons: A Guide to the Basics. ISBN: 0830725350. Pages 47-48, 97-103, 117, 118.*

Ward, Lock A. *Nuevo Diccionario de la Biblia. Editorial Unilit: Miami, Florida, ISBN: 0-7899-0217-6, 1999.*

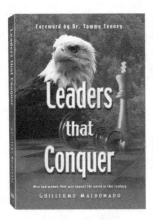
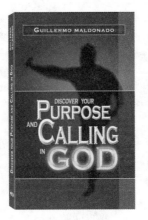

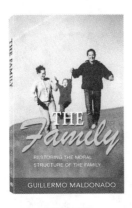
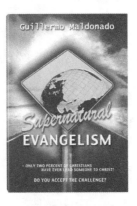

ERJ Publications

PRAYER

Guillermo Maldonado

ISBN-10: 1-59272-090-0
ISBN-13: 978-1-59272-090-3

OVERCOMING DEPRESSION

Guillermo Maldonado

ISBN-10: 1-59272-041-2
ISBN-13: 978-1-59272-041-5

SPIRITUAL MATURITY

Guillermo Maldonado

ISBN-10: 1-59272-163-X
ISBN-13: 978-1-59272-163-4
COMING SOON!

THE NEW WINE GENERATION

Guillermo Maldonado

ISBN-10: 1-59272-039-0
ISBN-13: 978-1-59272-039-2

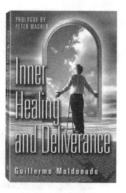

**INNER HEALING
AND DELIVERANCE**

Guillermo Maldonado

ISBN-10: 1-59272-007-2
ISBN-13: 978-1-59272-007-1

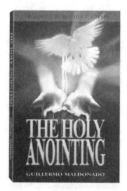

THE HOLY ANOINTING

Guillermo Maldonado

ISBN-10: 1-59272-038-2
ISBN-13: 978-1-59272-038-5

ERJ Publications

OUR
VISION

Taking the Word of God to the ends of the earth.

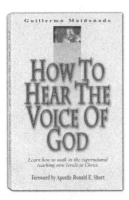

**HOW TO HEAR THE
VOICE OF GOD**

Guillermo Maldonado

ISBN-10: 1-59272-091-9
ISBN-13: 978-1-59272-091-0

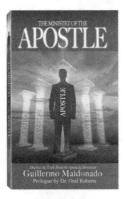

**THE MINISTRY
OF THE APOSTLE**

Guillermo Maldonado

ISBN-10: 1-59272-236-9
ISBN-13: 978-1-59272-236-5

**THE KINGDOM OF GOD
AND ITS RIGHTEOUSNESS**

Guillermo Maldonado

ISBN-10: 1-59272-266-0
ISBN-13: 978-1-59272-266-2

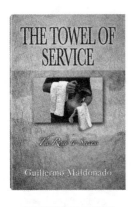

THE TOWEL OF SERVICE

Guillermo Maldonado

ISBN-10: 1-59272-228-8
ISBN-13: 978-1-59272-228-0

**HOW TO RETURN
TO OUR FIRST LOVE**

Guillermo Maldonado

ISBN-10: 1-59272-162-1
ISBN-13: 978-1-59272-162-7

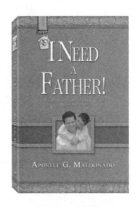

I NEED A FATHER

Guillermo Maldonado

ISBN-10: 1-59272-221-0
ISBN-13: 978-1-59272-221-1

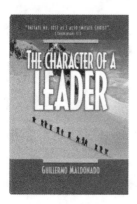
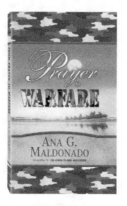
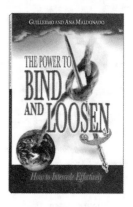